Sublime™

Using Sublime's exquisite Italian baby dk yarn, made from the highest quality natural fibres, we have created yet another irresistible range of hand knits for your baby's wardrobe.

Each piece has been designed using Sublime baby cashmere merino silk dk. This reassuringly delicate, soft and smooth yarn is the gentlest, natural blend next to your baby's skin and it's machine washable too!

We have the prettiest of cardies for little girls in gorgeous sorbet colours, and sporty nautical knits for little boys with jolly hats in blues and stones. Lots of irresistible knits for all those special days and holidays – or simply to look gorgeous every day.

Sublime baby hand knits – for the very best dressed babies around.

The most deliciously pretty
cardie for those special
occasions when a little girl
needs to be noticed.
Rosy Posy Cardie

If you like to keep it simple here's
the knit for you. Try the edging in
one of our pretty cupcake colours
– they'll look so sweet!
Little Sorbet Cardie

Just a Sublime little detail...
Seaside Vest

You won't be tied in knots with this
one – we give fab instructions and it's
only a little knit – go on give it a try!
Little Big Cable

A very dapper waistcoat –
the perfect accompaniment
to smart boy's linen shorts
and shirt.
Seaside Vest

Easy to make in simple knit and
purl stitches – won't he look ship
shape on the sea shore!
Little Anchor Man

The sleep anywhere blanket – perfect
for snuggling up in the prambuggy,
car seat or on the plane.
Ziggy Blanket

This trusty little hat will go with
everything – especially big blue eyes!
Little Anchor Beanie
Blue Anchor Man

Team this cardie with his fave t-shirt for
splashing around on the seashore in his first
wellie boots!
Seaside Cardie

CONTENTS

ESSENTIAL INFORMATION

Tension

Please take a little time to knit a tension square of the size indicated for the design you are working. If it's smaller your tension is tight and the garment will be small when completed. If it's bigger your tension is loose and the garment will be big when completed. Knitting a garment at an incorrect tension will produce disappointing results and may well require a different amount of yarn than we specified. Try another tension square on a bigger needle if your first square was small, or smaller needles if your first square was big.

When your square measures 10cm, (4in) begin knitting the garment on the needles you used for this square. If you have had to change your needle size, remember that if the design uses more than one size of needle you will need to adjust each needle size.

Sizing

Instructions are given for the first size. The figures within the brackets refer to the larger sizes. Where only one figure is given this applies to all the sizes.

Yarn amounts

The yarn amounts given for each design are based on average requirements when using the correct yarn and tension.

Finishing your garment

When sewing up your garment please take care and a little bit of time to follow the instructions given with each design. We suggest that you use mattress stitch for vertical seams and the grafting technique for horizontal or shoulder seams shown below to give it a neater finish.

Joining horizontal or shoulder seams.

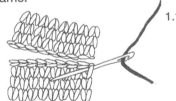

1.1 Lay the pieces to be sewn edge to edge. Starting at the right hand side of work bring the needle up through the centre of the first stitch of the lower piece as shown in diagram 1.1.

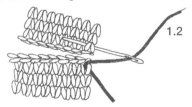

1.2 Pass the needle under both strands of the first stitch of the upper piece (emerging between the first and second stitches of the upper piece) as shown in diagram 1.2.

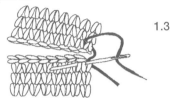

1.3 Then take the needle back into the centre of the first stitch on the lower piece and emerging up through the centre of the next stitch to the left as shown in diagram 1.3.

* On the upper piece take the needle down behind the first two strands of the next stitch to the left. Then crossing to the lower piece take the needle down through the centre of the last stitch worked emerging through the centre of the next stitch. * Repeat from * to * to end.

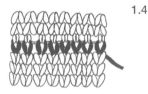

Diagram 1.4 shows a finished seam, with the dark thread representing the stitched row.

These examples show stocking stitch pieces sewn together, but the principle is the same for any knitted fabric.

Joining vertical seams (i.e. side or sleeve seams)

Mattress stitch

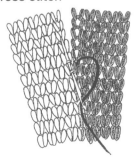

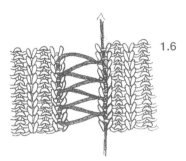

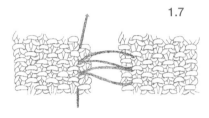

With right side of work facing lay the two pieces to be joined flat and edge to edge. Working from the front and either one stitch or half a stitch in from the edge on each piece, depending on what fabric you are sewing together, insert the needle from the front through the centre of stitch sliding it under two rows as illustrated in 1.5, 1.6 and 1.7. (We recommend that you take a full stitch from each side when joining garter stitch and moss stitch, but only half a stitch when joining stocking stitch or ribbed patterns). Cross to the opposite piece of work and slide the needle under two rows at a time. Repeat this action. Make sure that you don't miss any rows and that the work matches at both sides.

Once the garment is complete place a damp cloth over a thick towel. Place the garment onto the damp cloth. Pin out the garment to the measurements given, making sure that enough pins are used so that the outline of the garment remains smooth. Cover with damp cloths and leave to dry naturally.

Washing Instructions

Check the ball band for the washing instructions. After washing reshape while still wet and dry flat away from direct heat.

SUBLIME™ CANNOT ACCEPT RESPONSIBILITY FOR THE RESULT OF USING ANY OTHER YARN.

Rosy Posy Cardie, Sunflower Cardi, Rosy Posy Hat, Alice Band, Little Petal Alice Band and Sunflower Alice Band

worked in Sublime baby cashmere merino silk dk

You will also need 1 Pair of 4mm (UK8 – USA6) Knitting Needles for your main knitting (or the size required to give the correct tension). 1 Pair of 3¼mm (UK10 – USA3) Knitting Needles for border and yoke (or a needle 2 sizes smaller than you use for the main knitting). 1 Button.

SIZES

Age	0-6 months	6-12 months	1-2 years	2-3 years	
To Fit Chest	41	46	51	56	cm
	16	18	20	22	in
Actual Size	45	51	56	62	cm
	17¾	20	22	24½	in
Full Length	21	25	29	35	cm
(approximately)	8¼	9¾	11½	13¾	in
Rosy Posy Cardie					
Sleeve length (adjustable)	15	17	20	24	cm
	6	6½	8	9½	in
Sunflower Cardie					
Sleeve length	1	1	1	1	cm
	½	½	½	½	in

Rosy Posy Hat To fit an average size baby's head for the age indicated.
Alice Band To fit an average size baby's head for the age indicated.
Sunflower To fit an average size baby's head for the age indicated.
Little Petal Alice To fit an average size baby's head for the age indicated.

MATERIALS

	0-6	6-12	1-2	2-3	
Rosy Posy Cardie					
K001 Sublime baby cashmere merino silk dk shade 121 mousse	2	3	4	4	50g balls
Sunflower Cardie					
K001 Sublime baby cashmere merino silk dk shade 05 waterlily	2	2	3	3	50g balls
Rosy Posy Hat					
K001 Sublime baby cashmere merino silk dk					
shade 121 mousse for main	1	1	1	1	50g ball
shade 05 waterlily for contrast A	1	1	1	1	50g ball
shade 101 custard for contrast B	1	1	1	1	50g ball
Alice Head Band					
K001 Sublime baby cashmere merino silk dk					
shade 121 mousse	1	1	1	1	50g ball
Sunflower Alice Band					
K001 Sublime baby cashmere merino silk dk					
shade 05 waterlily for main	1	1	1	1	50g ball
shade 101 custard for contrast	1	1	1	1	50g ball
Little Petal Alice Band					
K001 Sublime baby cashmere merino silk dk					
shade 122 honey bunny	1	1	1	1	50g ball

TENSION

Please take a little time now to knit a stocking stitch tension square. **Using 4mm needles cast on 22 sts and work 28 rows in stocking stitch (1 row knit, 1 row purl). This should now measure 10cm, (4in) square.** If your square isn't the correct width please refer to page 2.

ABBREVIATIONS

C contrast, **cm** centimetres, **DK** double knitting, **g** grammes, **in** inch(es), **k** knit, **M** main, **mm** millimetres, **0** no rows, **p** purl, **st(s)** stitch(es), **tog** together.
K2tog insert the the right hand needle through the 2nd and 1st stitches on the left hand needle and knit them together to form a single stitch.
P2tog insert the the right hand needle purlways through the 1st and 2nd stitches on the left hand needle and purl them together to form a single stitch.
Psso pass slipped stitch over – pass the slipped stitch from the right hand needle over the stitch you have just worked.
S1 slip 1 stitch knitways – insert the needle into the next stitch as if to knit but just slip it off the left hand needle onto the right hand needle without working.

Circle the size you wish to make

ROSY POSY CARDIE
BACK

Using your smaller needles cast on 50 [56: 62:68] sts.
1st Row (this will be the right side of the work - **rs**). Knit to end.
This row will now be referred to as garter stitch.
Work 3 rows in garter stitch.
Change to your main needles and beginning with a knit row work in stocking stitch for the remainder of the back as follows:-
Work until the back measures 9 [12:15:20] cm, (3½ [4¾:6:8]in), finishing after a purl row

so that the right side of the work faces you for the beginning of the raglan shaping. The back should measure approximately 23 [26: 28:31]cm, (9 [10¼:11:12]in) across at this point.

Shape Raglan

Cast off 4 sts at beginning of the next 2 rows. You will now have 42 [48:54:60] sts on the needle.

For 1st, 2nd and 3rd sizes only

Work 6 [10:10] rows decreasing 1 st at each end of 3rd and every following 0 [4th:4th] row. You will now have 40 [44:50] sts on the needle.

For 4th size only

Work 2 rows straight.

For all 4 sizes

Work 6 [4:6:14] rows decreasing 1 st at each end of 1st and every following alternate row. You will now have 34 [40:44:46] sts on the needle.
Cast off remaining 34 [40:44:46] sts **loosely**.

LEFT FRONT

Using your smaller needles cast on 28 [30: 34:36] sts.
Work 3 rows in garter stitch.
Next Row. K4, leave these sts on a safety pin, knit to end. You will know have 24 [26:30:32] sts on the needle.
Change to your main needles and work in stocking stitch until left front measures same as the back to shape raglan, finishing after a purl row.

Shape Raglan and Neck

Next Row. Cast off 4 sts (raglan edge), knit to end. You will now have 20 [22:26:28] sts on the needle.
Next Row. Cast off 3 [3:4:4] sts purlways (neck edge), purl to end. You will now have 17 [19:22:24] sts on the needle.

Next Row. Knit.
Next Row. Cast off 3 [3:4:4] sts purlways, purl to end. You will now have 14 [16:18:20] sts on the needle.

For 1st, 2nd and 3rd sizes only

Work 4 [8:8] rows decreasing 1 st at raglan edge in 1st and following 0 [4th:4th] row AT SAME TIME decreasing 1 st at neck edge in every row. You will now have 9 [6:8] sts on the needle.

For 1st size only

Work 2 rows decreasing 1 st at raglan edge in 1st row AT SAME TIME decreasing 1 st at neck edge in every row. You will now have 6 sts on the needle.

For 4th size only

Work 8 rows decreasing 1 st at raglan edge in 1st and every following alternate row AT SAME TIME decreasing 1 st at neck edge in every row. You will now have [8] sts on the needle.

For all 4 sizes

Work 3 [3:5:5] rows decreasing 1 st at each end of 1st and every following alternate row. You will now have 2 sts on the needle.
Next Row. P2tog. Fasten off.

LEFT FRONT BORDER

With right side of work facing, using your smaller needles cast on 1 st (cast on stitch to be used for sewing border to front), using same yarn knit 4 sts left on a safety pin. You will now have 5 sts on the needle.
Next Row. S1, k4.
Work in garter stitch as set until border is of sufficient length when slightly stretched to go up left front, finishing after a wrong side row. Leave these 5 sts on a safety pin. Sew border in position evenly along left front using cast on st.

RIGHT FRONT

Using your smaller needles cast on 28 [30:

34:36] sts.

Work 3 rows in garter stitch.

Next Row. Knit to last 4 sts, leave these 4 sts on a stitch holder. You will now have 24 [26: 30:32] sts on the needle.

Change to your main needles and work in stocking stitch until right front measures the same as the back to shape raglan, finishing after a knit row.

Shape Raglan and Neck

Next Row. Cast off 4 sts (raglan edge), purl to end. You will now have 20 [22:26:28] sts on the needle.

Next Row. Cast off 3 [3:4:4] sts (neck edge), knit to end. You will now have 17 [19:22:24] sts on the needle.

Next Row. Purl.

Next Row. Cast off 3 [3:4:4] sts, knit to end. You will now have 14 [16:18:20] sts on the needle.

Next Row. Purl.

For 1st, 2nd and 3rd sizes only

Work 4 [8:8] rows decreasing 1 st at neck edge in every row AT SAME TIME decreasing 1 st at raglan edge in 1st and following 0 [4th:4th] row. You will now have 9 [6:8] sts on the needle.

For 1st size only

Work 2 rows decreasing 1 st at neck edge in every row AT SAME TIME decreasing 1 st at raglan edge in 1st row. You will now have 6 sts on the needle.

For 4th size only

Work 8 rows decreasing 1 st at neck edge in every row AT SAME TIME decreasing 1 st at raglan edge in 1st and every following alternate row. You will now have [8] sts on the needle.

For all 4 sizes

Work 3 [3:5:5] rows decreasing 1 st at each end of 1st and every following alternate row.

You will now have 2 sts on the needle.

Next Row. P2tog. Fasten off.

RIGHT FRONT BORDER

With wrong side of work facing, using your smaller needles cast on 1 st (cast on stitch to be used for sewing border to front), using same yarn knit 4 sts left on a safety pin. You will now have 5 sts on the needle.

Next Row. S1, k4.

Work in garter stitch as set until border is of sufficient length when slightly stretched to go up right front, finishing after a wrong side row. Do not break off yarn. Leave these 5 sts on a safety pin. Sew border in position along right front using cast on st.

LONG SLEEVES (Both alike)

Using your smaller needles cast on 36 [36: 38:40] sts, work 4 rows in garter stitch.

Change to your main needles and beginning with a knit row work in stocking stitch for the remainder of the sleeve as follows:-

Work 10 [10:10:2] rows.

Work 19 [25:33:51] rows increasing 1 st at each end of 1st and every following 18th [8th: 8th:10th] row (there will be 17 [7:7:9] rows straight between each increase row). You will now have 40 [44:48:52] sts on the needle. Continue without further shaping until sleeve is 15 [17:20:24]cm, (6 [6½:8:9½]in), finishing after a purl row.

Shape Raglan

Cast off 4 sts at beginning of the next 2 rows. You will now have 32 [36:40:44] sts on the needle.

Work 2 rows without shaping.

Work [10:12:14:14] rows decreasing 1 st at each end of 1st and every following 4th row. You will now have 26 [30:32:36] sts on the needle.

Cast off remaining 26 [30:32:36] sts **loosely**.

YOKE

Join raglan seams. With rs facing, using your

smaller needles work across 5 sts of right front border as follows:- k3, k2tog, pick up and knit 15 [18:21:23] sts evenly along right side of neck, 26 [30:32:36] sts at top of right sleeve, 34 [40:44:46] sts from cast off sts at back, 26 [30:32:36] sts from cast off sts at top of left sleeve, 15 [18:21:23] sts evenly along left side of neck and work across 5 sts of left front border as follows:- k2tog, k3. You will now have 124 [144:158:172] sts on the needle.

Work 5 [5:7:7] rows in garter stitch.

Next Row. (decrease row) K5 [5:8:5], k2tog, (k5, k2tog) 16 [19:20:23] times, k5 [4:8:4]. You will now have 107 [124:137:148] sts on the needle.

Work 5 [5:7:7] rows in garter stitch.

Next Row. (decrease row) K5 [4:8:4], k2tog, (k4, k2tog) 16 [19:20:23] times, k4 [4:7:4]. You will now have 90 [104:116:124] sts on the needle.

Work 5 [5:7:7] rows in garter stitch.

Next Row. (decrease row) K4 [4:7:4], k2tog, (k3, k2tog) 16 [19:20:23] times, k4 [3:7:3]. You will now have 73 [84:95:100] sts on the needle.

Work 3 rows in garter stitch.

Next Row. (decrease row) K3, (yfwd, k2tog) buttonhole, k0 [1:3:1], (k2, k2tog) 16 [19: 20:23] times, k4 [2: 7:2]. You will now have 57 [65:75:77] sts on the needle.

Work 4 rows in garter stitch.

Cast off.

FLOWERS

Flower A (make 4 [5:5:5])

Petals

Using your smaller needles and main cast on 60 sts.

1st Row. (K1, cast off 8 sts) 6 times. 12 sts. Break of yarn, run yarn through remaining 12 sts, draw up and fasten off.

Flower Centre

Using your smaller needles and contrast cast on 1 st.

1st Row. (K1, p1, k1, p1, k1) into 1st st. You will now have 5 sts on the needle.
2nd Row. Purl.
3rd Row. Knit.
4th Row. P2tog, p1, p2tog. You will now have 3 sts on the needle.
5th Row. S1, k2tog, psso. You will now have 1 st on the needle.
Break off yarn, fasten off.

Flower B (Make 4 [5:5:5])
Petals
Using contrast instead of main work as given for petals of Flower A.

Flower Centre
Using main instead of contrast work as given for centre of Flower A.

Flower C (Make 4 [5:5:5])
Petals
Using your smaller needles and main cast on 60 sts.
1st Row. Using contrast (K1, cast off 8 sts) 6 times. 12 sts.
Break of yarn, run yarn through remaining 12 sts, draw up and fasten off.

TO MAKE UP
Join side and sleeve seams. Sew on button. Sew flower centres to petals. Sew flowers in position around start of yoke as shown in photograph. Pin out garment to the measurement given. Cover with damp cloths and leave until dry (refer to page 2). See ball band for washing and further care instructions.

SUNFLOWER CARDIE
BACK
Work the back as given for Back of Rosy Posy Cardie.

LEFT FRONT
Work the left front as given for Left Front of Rosy Posy Cardie.

RIGHT FRONT
Work the right front as given for Right Front of Rosy Posy Cardie.

SLEEVES (Both alike)
Using your smaller needles cast on 36 [40:44:48] sts, work 3 rows garter stitch.
Next Row. K2 [4:5:4], inc in next st, (k9 [9:10:12], inc in next st) 3 times, k3 [5:5:4]. You will now have 40 [44:48:52] sts on the needle.
Change to your main needles and beginning with a knit row continue in stocking stitch for the remainder of the sleeve as follows:-

Shape Raglan
Work raglan shapings as given for Shape Raglan of Rosy Posy Sleeves.

YOKE
Work the yoke as given for Yoke of Rosy Posy Cardie.

FLOWERS
Using 1 colour only make 8 [11:11:11] flowers as given for Flower A on Rosy Posy Cardi.

TO MAKE UP
Work to make up as given for to make up of Rosy Posy Cardie.

ROSY POSY HAT
Using your smaller needles cast on 79 [85:95:101] sts. Work in garter stitch until hat measures 8 [9:10:11]cm, (3 [3½:4:4¼]in), finishing after a right side row.
Next Row (decrease row). K9 [7:6:9], k2tog, (k10 [12:7:7], k2tog) 5 [5:9:9] times, k8 [6:6:9]. You will now have 73 [79:85:91] sts on the needle.
Change to your main needles and work 4 rows in stocking stitch.

Shape Crown
1st Row. K1, (k2tog, k4) 12 [13:14:15] times. You will now have 61 [66:71:76] sts on the needle.
Work 3 rows in stocking stitch.
5th Row. K1, (k2tog, k3) 12 [13:14:15] times. You will now have 49 [53:57:61] sts on the needle.
Work 3 rows in stocking stitch.
9th Row. K1, (k2tog, k2) 12 [13:14:15] times. You will now have 37 [40:43:46] sts on the needle.
Work 3 rows in stocking stitch.
13th Row. K1, (k2tog, k1) 12 [13:14:15] times. You will now have 25 [27:29:31] sts on the needle.
Work 3 rows in stocking stitch.
17th Row. K1, (k2tog) 12 [13:14:15] times. You will now have 13 [14:15:16] sts on the needle.
Break off yarn, run yarn through remaining 13 [14:15:16] sts, draw up and fasten off.

FLOWERS
Work 1 flower each in Flower A, Flower B and Flower C as given for Rosy Posy Cardi.

TO MAKE UP
Join back seam. Sew flower centres to petals. Sew flowers in position to hat as shown in photograph. Cover with damp cloths and leave until dry (refer to page 2). See ball band for washing and further care instructions.

ALICE HEADBAND
Using your smaller needles cast on 10 sts.
1st Row. (this will be the right side of the work - **rs**). S1, knit to end.
1st row forms garter stitch.
Repeat it until band measures 33 [36:38:41]cm, (13 [14:15:16]in), or length required (when slightly stretched), finishing after a right side row.
Cast off.

TO MAKE UP
Join cast on and cast off edges together. Cover with a damp cloth until dry (refer to page 2). See ball band for washing and care instructions.

SUNFLOWER ALICE BAND

Using your smaller needles and main yarn cast on 10 sts.

1st Row. (this will be the right side of the work - **rs**) S1, knit to end.
1st row forms garter stitch.
Repeat it until band measures 33 [36: 38:41]cm, (13 [14:15:16]in), or length required (when slightly stretched), finishing after a right side row.
Cast off.

FLOWERS

Work 1 flower each in Flower A, Flower B and Flower C as given for Rosy Posy Cardi.

TO MAKE UP

Join cast on and cast off edges together. Sew flower centres to petals. Sew flowers in position to band as shown in photograph. Cover with damp cloths and leave until dry (refer to page 2). See ball band for washing and further care instructions.

LITTLE PETAL ALICE BAND

Using your smaller needles cast on 10 sts.

1st Row. (this will be the right side of the work - **rs**) S1, knit to end.
1st row forms garter stitch.
Repeat it until band measures 33 [36: 38:41]cm, (13 [14:15:16]in), or length required (when slightly stretched), finishing after a right side row.
Cast off.

FLOWERS

Using one colour only work 3 flowers as given for Flower A on Rosy Posy Cardi.

TO MAKE UP

Join cast on and cast off edges together. Sew flower centres to petals. Sew flowers in position to band as shown in photograph. Cover with damp cloths and leave until dry (refer to page 2). See ball band for washing and further care instructions.

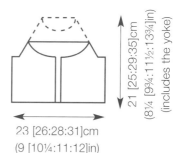

21 [25:29:35]cm
(8¼ [9¾:11½:13¾]in) (includes the yoke)

23 [26:28:31]cm
(9 [10¼:11:12]in)

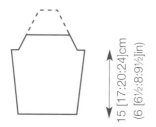

15 [17:20:24]cm
(6 [6½:8:9½]in)

1cm
(½in)

Sublime™

Little Sorbet and Peach Sorbet Cardies

worked in Sublime baby cashmere merino silk dk

You will also need
1 pair of 4mm (UK8 – USA6) Knitting Needles for the main knitting (or the size required to give the correct tension).
1 pair of 3¼mm (UK10 – USA3) Knitting Needles for the borders (or a needle 2 sizes smaller than you use for the main knitting).

TENSION
Please take a little time now to knit a tension square. **Using 4mm needles cast on 22 stitches and work 28 rows in stocking stitch (1 row knit, 1 row purl). This should now measure 10cm, (4in) square.** If your square isnt the correct width please refer to page 2.

SIZES

Age	0-6 months	6-12 months	1-2 years	2-3 years	
To Fit Chest	41	46	51	56	cm
	16	18	20	22	in
Actual Size	41	46	51	56	cm
	16	8	20	22	in
Full Length	22	24	26	28	cm
	8¾	9½	10¼	11	in
Sleeve Length	15	17	20	24	cm
Peach Sorbet	6	6½	8	9½	in
Little Sorbet	1	1	1	1	cm
	½	½	½	½	in

MATERIALS

Little Sorbet Cardie					
K001 Sublime baby cashmere merino silk dk shade 121 mousse for main shade 126 rosy or	1	2	2	2	50g balls
122 honey bunny for contrast	1	1	1	1	50g balls
Peach Sorbet Cardie					
K001 Sublime baby cashmere merino silk dk shade 122 honey bunny	2	3	3	3	50g balls

ABBREVIATIONS
cm centimetres, **dec** decrease(ing), **dk** double knitting, **g** grammes, **in** inch(es), **inc** increase(ing), **k** knit, **mm** millimetres, **p** purl, **0** no rows, **rep** repeat, **st(s)** stitch(es), **tog** together.
K2tog insert the right hand needle through the 2nd and 1st stitches on the left hand needle and knit them together to form a single stitch.
P2tog insert the right hand needle purlways through the 1st and 2nd stitches on the left hand needle and purl them together to form a single stitch.

Circle the size you wish to make

LITTLE SORBET CARDIE
BACK
Using your smaller needles and contrast yarn cast on 54 [62:66:70] sts.

2x2 rib
1st Row (this will be the right side of work - **rs**).
K2, * p2, k2, rep from * to end.
2nd Row. * P2, k2, rep from * to last 2 sts, p2.
These 2 rows form 2x2 rib.

Work 3 rows in 2x2 rib.
6th Row. (decrease row) P2 [5:4:2], p2tog, (p4 [3:5:6], p2tog) 8 [10:8:8] times, p2 [5:4:2]. You will now have 45 [51:57:61] sts on the needle.
Change to your main needles and using main yarn and beginning with a knit row work in stocking stitch for the remainder of the back as follows:-
Work until back measures 11 [12:13:14]cm, (4¼ [4¾:5¼:5½]in), finishing after a purl row so that the right side of work faces you for the beginning of the armhole shaping.
The back should measure approximately 21 [23:26:28]cm, (8¼ [9:10¼:11]in) across at this point.

Shape Raglan Armhole
Cast off 4 sts at beginning of next 2 rows. You will now have 37 [43:49:53] sts on the needle.

For 1st and 2nd sizes only
Work 4 rows dec 1 st at each end of 1st row. You will now have 35 [41] sts on the needle.

For 4th size only
Work 4 rows dec 1 st at each end of every row. You will now have [45] sts on the needle.

For all 4 sizes
Work 10 [14:20:16] rows dec 1 st at each end of 1st and every following alternate row. You will now have 25 [27:29:29] sts on the needle. Cast off remaining 25 [27:29:29] sts.

LEFT FRONT
Using your smaller needles and contrast yarn cast on 23 [27:31:31] sts.

Rib
1st Row (this will be the right side of work - **rs**). K2, * p2, k2, rep from * to last st, p1.
2nd Row K1, * p2, k2, rep from * to last 2 sts, p2.
These 2 rows form rib.
Work 3 rows in rib.
6th Row. (decrease row) P2 [2:2:6], p2tog, (p2, p2tog) 4 [5:6:4] times, p3 [3:3:7].
You will now have 18 [21:24:26] sts on the needle.
Change to your main needles and using main yarn beginning with a knit row work in stocking stitch for the remainder of the left front as follows:-
Continue until left front measures same as Back to armhole, finishing after a purl row.

Shape Raglan Armhole
Next Row. Cast off 4 sts, knit to end. You will now have 14 [17:20:22] sts on the needle.
Next Row. Purl.

For 1st and 2nd sizes only
Work 4 rows dec 1 st at raglan edge in 1st row. You will now have 13 [16] sts on the needle.

For 4th size only
Work 4 rows dec 1 st at raglan edge in every row. You will now have [18] sts on the needle.

For all 4 sizes
Work 3 [7:13:9] rows dec 1 st at raglan edge in 1st and every following alternate row. You will now have 11 [12:13:13] sts on the needle.

Neck Shaping
Next Row. Cast off 3 [4:5:5] sts, purl to end. You will now have 8 sts on the needle.
Work 3 rows dec 1 st at raglan edge in 1st and following alternate row AT SAME TIME dec 1 st at neck edge in every row. You will now have 3 sts on the needle.
Next Row. Purl.
Next Row. K2tog, k1. You will now have 2 sts on the needle.
Next Row. P2tog. Fasten off.

RIGHT FRONT
Using your smaller needles and contrast yarn cast on 23 [27:31:31] sts.

Rib
1st Row (this will be the right side of work - **rs**). P1, k2, * p2, k2, rep from * to end.
2nd Row. * P2, k2, rep from * to last 3 sts, p2, k1.
These 2 rows form rib.
Work 3 rows in rib.
6th Row. (decrease row) P3 [3:3:7], p2tog, (p2, p2tog) 4 [5:6:4] times, p2 [2:2:6].
You will now have 18 [21:24:26] sts on the needle.
Change to your main needles and using main yarn beginning with a knit row work in stocking stitch for the remainder of the right front as follows:-
Continue until right front measures same as Back to armhole, finishing after a knit row.

Shape Raglan Armhole
Next Row. Cast off 4 sts, purl to end. You will now have 14 [17:20:22] sts on the needle.
For 1st and 2nd sizes only
Work 4 rows dec 1 st at raglan edge in 1st row. You will now have 13 [16] sts on the needle.

For 4th size only
Work 4 rows dec 1 st at raglan edge in every row. You will now have [18] sts on the needle.

For all 4 sizes
Work 2 [6:12:8] rows dec 1 st at raglan edge in 1st and every following 0 [2nd:2nd:2nd] row. You will now have 12 [13:14:14] sts on the needle.

Neck Shaping
Next Row. Cast off 3 [4:5:5] sts, knit to last 2 sts, k2tog. You will now have 8 sts on the needle.
Next Row. Purl.
Work 3 rows dec 1 st at neck edge in every row AT SAME TIME dec 1 st at raglan edge in 1st and following alternate row. You will now have 3 sts on the needle.
Next Row. Purl.
Next Row. K1, k2tog. You will now have 2 sts on the needle.
Next Row. P2tog. Fasten off.

SLEEVES (Both alike)
Using your smaller needles and contrast yarn cast on 34 [38:42:46] sts, work 3 rows in 2x2 rib.
4th Row (increase row). Purl to end inc 3 sts evenly across row. You will now have 37 [41:45:49] sts on the needle.
Change to your main needles and using main yarn and beginning with a knit row work in stocking stitch for the remainder of the sleeve as follows:-

Shape Raglan
Cast off 4 sts at beginning of next 2 rows. You will now have 29 [33:37:41] sts on the needle.
Work 14 [18:12:12] rows dec 1 st at each end of 1st and every following 6th [4th:4th:4th] row. You will now have 23 [23:31:35] sts on the needle.

For 3rd and 4th sizes only
Work 8 rows dec 1 st at each end of 1st and

every following alternate row. You will now have [23:27] sts on the needle.

For all 4 sizes
Cast off remaining 23 [23:23:27] sts.

RIGHT FRONT BORDER
With right side of the work facing you, using your smaller needles and contrast yarn pick up and knit 4 sts evenly up rib and 31 [35:39:43] sts evenly up front edge, ending at cast off sts of neck.
You will now have 35 [39:43:47] sts on the needle.
1st Row. K1, * p2, k2, rep from * to last 2 sts, p2.
2nd Row. K2, * p2, k2, rep from * to last st, p1.
These 2 rows form rib.
Work 3 rows in rib.
Cast off in rib.

LEFT FRONT BORDER
With right side of the work facing you, using your smaller needles and contrast yarn, starting at cast off sts at neck pick up and knit 31 [35:39:43] sts evenly down front edge and 4 sts evenly down rib.
You will now have 35 [39:43:47] sts on the needle.
1st Row. * P2, k2, rep from * to last 3 sts, p2, k1.
2nd Row. P1, k2, * p2, k2, rep from * to end.
These 2 rows form rib.
Work 3 rows in rib.
Cast off in rib.

NECKBAND
Join raglan seams then using your smaller needles and contrast yarn pick up sts around neck shaping as follows:- Cast on 30 [30: 32:34] sts, with right side of the work facing you, using same needle and yarn pick up and knit 4 sts evenly along border, 7 [8:9:9] sts evenly up right side of neck, 17 [17:17:21] sts from 23 [23:23:27] cast off sts at top of right

sleeve, 22 [24:26:26] sts from 25 [27:29:29] cast off sts at back of neck, 17 [17:17:21] sts from 23 [23:23:27] cast off sts at top of left sleeve, 7 [8:9:9] sts evenly down left side of neck, 4 sts evenly along edge of border and cast on 30 [30:32:34] sts. You will now have 138 [142:150:162] sts on the needle.
Starting with 2nd row of 2x2 rib work 5 rows.
Cast off in rib.

TO MAKE UP
Join side and sleeve seams. Pin out garment to the measurement given and cover with damp cloths until dry (refer to page 2). See ball band for washing and further care instructions.

PEACH SORBET CARDIE
BACK
Work the back as given for the Back of Little Sorbet Cardie using one colour only.

LEFT FRONT
Work the left front as given for the Left Front of Little Sorbet Cardie using one colour only.

RIGHT FRONT
Work the right front as given for the Right Front of Little Sorbet Cardie using one colour only.

SLEEVES (Both alike)
Using your smaller needles cast on 34 [34: 38:38] sts, work 5 rows in 2x2 rib.
6th Row. Purl to end dec 1 st in centre of row for 1st and 3rd sizes only and inc 1 st in centre of row for 2nd and 4th sizes only. You will now have 33 [35:37:39] sts on the needle. Change to your main needles and beginning with a knit row work in stocking stitch for the remainder of the sleeve as follows:-
Work 15 [35:9:43] rows inc 1 st at each end of 3rd and every following 12th [8th:6th:8th] row (there will be 11 [7:5:7] rows straight between each increase row).
You will now have 37 [45:41:51] sts on the needle.

For 1st, 3rd and 4th sizes only
Work 14 [32:10] rows inc 1 st at each end of 14th [8th:10th] and every following 0 [8th:0] row (there will be 13 [7:9] rows straight between each increase row). You will now have 39 [49:53] sts on the needle.

For all 4 sizes
Work without further shaping until the sleeve is 15 [17:20:24]cm, (6 [6½:8:9½]in), finishing after a purl row.

Shape Raglan
Cast off 4 sts at beginning of next 2 rows. You will now have 31 [37:41:45] sts on the needle.
Work 14 [8:4:4] rows dec 1 st at each end of 1st and every following 4th [4th:0:0] row. You will now have 23 [33:39:43] sts on the needle.

For 2nd, 3rd and 4th sizes only
Work [10:16:16] rows dec 1 st at each end of 1st and every following alternate row.
You will now have [23:23:27] sts on the needle.

For all 4 sizes
Cast off remaining 23 [23:23:27] sts.

RIGHT FRONT BORDER
Work the right front border as given for the Right Front Border of Little Sorbet Cardie using one colour only.

LEFT FRONT BORDER
Work the left front border as given for the Left Front Border of Little Sorbet Cardie using one colour only.

NECKBAND
Work the neckband as given for the Neckband of Little Sorbet Cardie using one colour only.

TO MAKE UP
Work to make up as given for the To Make Up of Little Sorbet Cardie.

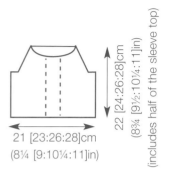

22 [24:26:28]cm
(8¾ [9½:10¼:11]in)
(includes half of the sleeve top)

21 [23:26:28]cm
(8¼ [9:10¼:11]in)

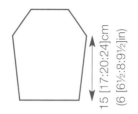

15 [17:20:24]cm
(6 [6½:8:9½]in)

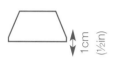

1cm
(½in)

Sublime™

Seaside Cardi and Seaside Vest

worked in Sublime baby
cashmere merino silk dk

SIZES

Age	0-6 months	6-12 months	1-2 years	2-3 years	
To Fit Chest	41	46	51	56	cm
	16	18	20	22	in
Actual size	45	50	55	61	cm
	17¾	19¾	21¾	24	in
Full Length (approximately)	24	28	32	38	cm
	9½	11	12½	15	in
Sleeve Length	15	17	20	24	cm
	6	6½	8	9½	in

MATERIALS

Seaside Cardi

K001 Sublime baby cashmere merino silk dk shade 06 pebble	3	3	4	5	50g balls

Seaside Vest

K001 Sublime baby cashmere merino silk dk shade 124 splash	2	2	3	3	50g balls

You will also need
1 pair of 4mm (UK8 – USA6) Knitting
Needles for the main knitting (or the size
required to give the correct tension).
1 pair of 3¾mm (UK9 – USA5) Knitting
Needles (larger needles) for the pattern (or a

needle 1 size smaller than you use for the
main knitting).
1 pair of 3¼mm (UK10 – USA3) Knitting
Needles (smaller needles) for rib and
armhole edgings on the waistcoat (or a
needle 2 sizes smaller than you use for the

main knitting).
4 buttons.

TENSION

Please take a little time now to knit a stocking stitch tension square. **Using 4mm needles cast on 22 stitches and work 28 rows in stocking stitch (1 row knit, 1 row purl). This should now measure 10cm, (4in) square.** If your square isn't the correct width please refer to page 2.

ABBREVIATIONS

cm centimetres, **dk** double knitting, **g** grammes, **in** inch(es), **k** knit, **mm** millimetres, **0** no rows, **st(s)** stitch(es), **tog** together.
K2tog insert the right hand needle through the 2nd and 1st stitches on the left hand needle and knit them together to form a single stitch.
Psso pass slipped stitch over – pass the slipped stitch from the right hand needle over the stitch or stitches you have just worked.
Yfwd bring yarn to front between needles then take yarn over the top of the right hand needle to form a single stitch.
S1 slip one stitch knitways – insert the right hand needle into next stitch as if to knit but just slip it off the left hand needle onto the right hand needle without working.

Circle the size you wish to make

SEASIDE CARDI
BACK

Regularly measure the width of the back as you knit. The Back should measure approximately 23 [25:28:32]cm, (9 [9¾: 11:12½]in) across.
Using your larger needles cast on 49 [55: 61:67] sts.

Pattern
** **1st Row** Knit (this will be the right side of the work –rs).

2nd Row. Knit.
3rd Row. Knit.
4th Row. Purl.
These 4 rows form pattern. **
Repeat them until back measures approximately 6 [7:8:10]cm (2½ [2¾:3:4]in) finishing after 4th row of pattern.***
Change to your main needles and beginning with a knit row work in stocking stitch for the remainder of the back as follows:-
Continue until back measures 24 [28: 32:38]cm, (9½ [11:12½:15]in), finishing after a purl row.

Shape Shoulders

Cast off 9 [10:11:12] sts at beginning of next 2 rows. You will now have 31 [35:39:43] sts on the needle.
Cast off 9 [10:11:13] sts at beginning of next 2 rows. You will now have 13 [15:17:17] sts on the needle.
Cast off remaining 13 [15:17:17] sts.

RIGHT FRONT

Using your larger needles cast on 27 [30: 33:36] sts.

Pattern
1st Row. (this will be the right side of the work –**rs**). S1, knit to end
2nd Row. Knit.
3rd Row. S1, knit to end.
4th Row. Purl.
These 4 rows form pattern.
Repeat them until right front measures approximately 6 [7:8:10]cm, (2½ [2¾:3:4]in) finishing after 4th row of pattern. **
Change to your main needles and beginning with a knit row work in stocking stitch for the remainder of the right front as follows:-
Continue until right front measures 14 [17: 20:25]cm, (5½ [6½:8:9¾]in) finishing after a purl row.

Neck Shaping
1st Row. K3, k2tog, knit to end. You will now

have 26 [29:32:35] sts on the needle.
2nd Row. Purl.
1st and 2nd rows set neck shaping.
Work 19 [23:27:27] rows decreasing 1 st at neck edge as before in 3rd and every following 4th row. You will now have 21 [23:25:28] sts on the needle.
Work on these 21 [23:25:28] sts until right front measures same as Back to shoulder shaping, finishing after a knit row.

Shape Shoulder
Next Row. Cast off 9 [10:11:12] sts, purl to end. You will now have 12 [13:14:16] sts on the needle.
Next Row. Knit.
Next Row. Cast off 9 [10:11:13] sts purl to end. You will now have 3 sts on the needle.
Next Row. Knit to end, cast on 1 st (cast on st to be used for sewing border to back of neck). You will now have 4 sts on the needle. Work on these 4 sts for back neck border as follows:-
Continue in stocking stitch until border is of sufficient length to fit halfway across back of neck, finishing after a purl row.
Cast off.
Mark the position for 4 buttons, the first one to be placed 4 rows up from the lower edge, the 4th one 1cm, (½in), below beginning of neck shaping and the other two evenly placed between these two.

LEFT FRONT

Using your larger needles cast on 27 [30: 33:36] sts.
Work from ** to ** as given for Back.
5th Row (Buttonhole row). Knit to last 5 sts, s1, k1, psso, yfwd, k3.
Starting with 2nd row of pattern work in pattern until left front measures approximately 6 [7:8:10]cm, (2½ [2¾:3:4]in), finishing after 4th row of pattern AT SAME TIME working

buttonholes to correspond with markers **.
Change to your main needles and beginning with a knit row work in stocking stitch for the remainder of the left front as follows:-
Continue until left front measures 14 [17: 20:25]cm (5½ [6½:8:9¾]in), finishing after a purl row AT SAME TIME working buttonholes to correspond with markers.

Neck Shaping
1st Row. Knit to last 5 sts, s1, k1, psso, k3. You will now have 26 [29:32:35] sts on the needle.
2nd Row. Purl.
1st and 2nd rows set neck shaping.
Work 19 [23:27:27] rows decreasing 1 st at neck edge as before in 3rd and every following 4th row. You will now have 21 [23:25:28] sts on the needle.
Work on these 21 [23:25:28] sts until left front measures same as Back to shoulder shaping, finishing after a purl row.

Shape Shoulder
Next Row. Cast off 9 [10:11:12] sts, knit to end. You will now have 12 [13:14:16] sts on the needle.
Next Row. Purl.
Next Row. Cast off 9 [10:11:13] sts, knit to end. You will now have 3 sts on the needle.
Next Row. Purl to end, cast on 1 st (cast on st to be used for sewing border to back of neck). You will now have 4 sts on the needle.
Work on these 4 sts for back neck border as follows:-
Continue in stocking stitch until border is of sufficient length to fit halfway across back of neck finishing after a purl row.
Cast off.

SLEEVES (Both alike)
Using your larger needles cast on 35 [35: 37:39] sts and work from ** to ** as given for

Back until sleeve measures approximately 5 [5: 6:8]cm, (2 [2:2½:3]in), finishing after 4th row of pattern.
Change to your main needles and beginning with a knit row work in stocking stitch for the remainder of the sleeve as follows:-
Work 23 [27:33:10] rows increasing 1 st at each end of 3rd and every following 10th [6th:6th:4th] row (there will be 9 [5:5:3] rows straight between each increase row). You will now have 41 [45:49:43] sts on the needle.

For 4th size only
Work 25 rows increasing 1 st at each end of 1st and every following 6th row (there will be 5 rows straight between each increase row). You will now have [53] sts on the needle.

For all 4 sizes
Work without further shaping until sleeve is 15 [17:20:24]cm, (6 [6½:8:9 ½]in), finishing after a purl row.

Shape Sleeve Top
Cast off 4 [5:3:3] sts at beginning of each of the next 4 [4:4:10] rows. You will now have 25 [25:37:23] sts on the needle.
Cast off 5 [5:4:4] sts at beginning of each of the next 4 [4:8:4] rows. You will now have 5 [5:5:7] sts on the needle.
Cast off remaining 5 [5:5:7] sts.

TAB
Using your smaller needles cast on 7 [9:11:13] sts and knit 3 rows.
Cast off.

TO MAKE UP
Join both shoulder seams. Fold sleeves in half lengthways then placing folds to shoulder seams, sew sleeves in position for approximately 10 [11:12:13]cm, (4 [4¼:4¾: 5¼]in), from top of shoulder. Join side and

sleeve seams. Join borders at back of neck and placing seam to centre back of neck sew border in position using cast on st. Sew tab in position on back. Sew on buttons. Pin out garment to the measurement given and cover with damp cloths until dry (refer to page 2). See ball band for washing and further care instructions.

SEASIDE VEST
BACK
Work back of the seaside vest as given for the Back of the Seaside Cardi to ***.
Change to your main needles and work the remainder of the back as follows:-
Work in stocking stitch until back measures 15 [18:21:26]cm, (6 [7:8¼:10¼]in), finishing after a purl row.

Shape Armholes
Cast off 2 [3:3:4] sts at beginning of next 2 rows. You will now have 45 [49:55:59] sts on the needle.
Work 2 [2:2:4] rows decreasing 1 st at each end of every row.
You will now have 41 [45:51:51] sts on the needle.
Work 3 [5:7:5] rows decreasing 1 st at each end of 1st and every following alternate row. You will now have 37 [39:43:45] sts on the needle.
Work without further shaping until armholes measure 9 [10:11:12]cm, (3½ [4:4¼:4¾]in), finishing after a purl row.

Shape Shoulders
Cast off 6 [6:6:7] sts at beginning of next 2 rows. You will now have 25 [27:31:31] sts on the needle.
Cast off 6 [6:7:7] sts at beginning of next 2 rows. You will now have 13 [15:17:17] sts on the needle.

RIGHT FRONT

Work the right front of the Seaside Vest as given for Right Front of Seaside Cardi to **.
Change to your main needles and beginning with a knit row work in stocking stitch for the remainder of the right front as follows:-
Continue until right front measures 4 rows less than Back to armhole shaping finishing after a purl row.

Neck Shaping

1st Row. K3, k2tog (neck edge), knit to end. You will now have 26 [29:32:35] sts on the needle.
1st row sets neck shaping.
2nd Row. Purl.
3rd Row. Knit.
4th Row. Purl.
5th Row. K3, k2tog, knit to end. You will now have 25 [28:31:34] sts on the needle.

Shape Armhole

Next Row. Cast off 2 [3:3:4] sts, purl to end. You will now have 23 [25:28:30] sts on the needle.
Work 2 [2:2:4] rows decreasing 1 st at neck edge as before in 0 [0:0:3rd] row AT SAME TIME decreasing 1 st at armhole edge in every row. You will now have 21 [23:26:25] sts on the needle.
Work 3 [5:7:5] rows decreasing 1 st at neck edge as before in 1st [1st:1st:3rd] and following 0 [4th:4th:0] row AT SAME TIME decreasing 1 st at armhole edge in 1st and every following alternate row. You will now have 18 [18:20:21] sts on the needle.
Work 10 [12:14:14] rows decreasing 1 st at neck edge only as before in 2nd [4th:2nd:2nd] and every following 4th row. You will now have 15 [15:16:17] sts on the needle.
Work without further shaping until right front armhole measures same as Back armhole finishing after a knit row.

Shape Shoulder

Next Row. Cast off 6 [6:6:7] sts, purl to end. You will now have 9 [9:10:10] sts on the needle.
Next Row. Knit.
Next Row. Cast off 6 [6:7:7] sts, purl to end. You will now have 3 sts on the needle.
Next Row. Knit to end, cast on 1 st (cast on st to be used for sewing border to back of neck). You will now have 4 sts on the needle. Work on these 4 sts for back neck border as follows:-
Continue in stocking stitch until border is of sufficient length to fit halfway across back of neck, finishing after a purl row.
Cast off.
Mark the position for 4 buttons the first one to be placed 4 rows up from the lower edge, the 4th one 1cm (½in) below beginning of neck shaping and the other two evenly placed between these two.

LEFT FRONT

Work the left front of Seaside Vest as given for Left Front of Seaside Cardi to **.
Change to your main needles and beginning with a knit row work in stocking stitch for the remainder of the left front as follows:-
Continue until left front measures 4 rows less than Back to armhole shaping finishing after a purl row AT SAME TIME working buttonholes to correspond with markers.

Neck Shaping

1st Row. Knit to last 5 sts, s1, k1, psso (neck edge), k3. You will now have 26 [29:32:35] sts on the needle.
1st row sets neck shaping.
2nd Row. Purl.
3rd Row. Knit.
4th Row. Purl.

Shape Armhole

Next Row. Cast off 2 [3:3:4] sts, knit to last 5 sts, s1, k1, psso, k3. You will now have 23 [25:28:30] sts on the needle.
Next Row. Purl.
Work 2 [2:2:4] rows decreasing 1 st at armhole edge in every row AT SAME TIME decreasing 1 st at neck edge as before in 0 [0: 0:3rd] row. You will now have 21 [23:26:25] sts on the needle.
Work 3 [5:7:5] rows decreasing 1 st at armhole edge in 1st and every following alternate row AT SAME TIME decreasing 1 st at neck edge as before in 1st [1st:1st:3rd] and every following 0 [4th:4th:0] row. You will now have 18 [18:20:21] sts on the needle.
Work 10 [12:14:14] rows decreasing 1 st at neck edge only as before in 2nd [4th:2nd:2nd] and every following 4th row. You will now have 15 [15:16:17] sts on the needle.
Work without further shaping until left front armhole measures same as Back armhole shaping, finishing after a purl row.

Shape Shoulder

Next Row. Cast off 6 [6:6:7] sts, knit to end. You will now have 9 [9:10:10] sts on the needle.
Next Row. Purl.
Next Row. Cast off 6 [6:7:7] sts, knit to end. You will now have 3 sts on the needle.
Next Row. Purl to end, cast on 1 st (cast on st to be used for sewing border to back of neck). You will now have 4 sts on the needle. Work on these 4 sts for back border as follows:-
Continue in stocking stitch until border is of sufficient length to fit halfway across back of neck, finishing after a purl row.
Cast off.

ARMHOLE EDGINGS (Both alike)

Join both shoulder seams with the right side of the work facing you, using your smaller needles pick up and knit 46 [50:56:60] sts evenly all round armhole edge.
Cast off knitways.

TAB

Using your smaller needles cast on 7 [9:11:13] sts and knit 3 rows.
Cast off.

TO MAKE UP

Join side and armhole edging seams. Join borders at back of neck and placing seam to centre back of neck sew border in position using cast on st. Sew tab in position to back.

Sew on buttons. Pin out garment to the measurement given and cover with damp cloths until dry (refer to page 2). See ball band for washing and further care instructions.

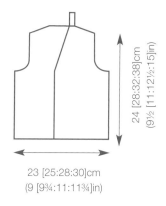

24 [28:32:38]cm
(9½ [11:12½:15]in)

23 [25:28:30]cm
(9 [9¾:11:11¾]in)

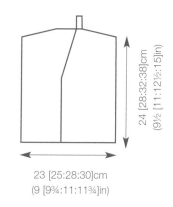

24 [28:32:38]cm
(9½ [11:12½:15]in)

23 [25:28:30]cm
(9 [9¾:11:11¾]in)

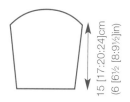

15 [17:20:24]cm
(6 [6½:8:9½]in)

Little Big Cable
worked in Sublime baby
cashmere merino silk dk

1 pair of 4mm (UK8 – USA6) Knitting
Needles for the main knitting (or the size
required to give the correct tension).
1 pair of 3¼mm (UK10 – USA3) Knitting
Needles for the ribs and neck edging (or
a needle 2 sizes smaller than you use
for the main knitting).
2 Stitch Holders and 3 Buttons.

TENSION
Please take a little time now to knit a
stocking stitch tension square. **Using 4mm
needles cast on 22 stitches and work 28
rows in reversed stocking stitch (1 row
purl, 1 row knit). This should now
measure 10cm, (4in) square.** If your
square isn't the correct width please refer
to page 2.

SIZES

Age	6-12 months	1-2 years	2-3 years	
To Fit Chest	46	51	56	cm
	18	20	22	in
Actual size	51	56	62	cm
	20	22	24½	in
Full Length	29	32	38	cm
(approximately)	11½	12½	15	in
Sleeve Length	17	20	24	cm
	6½	8	9½	in

MATERIALS
K001 Sublime baby cashmere merino silk dk

Shade 124 splash	3	4	5	50g balls

ABBREVIATIONS
cm centimetres, **dk** double knitting, **CN** cable
needle, **g** grammes, **in** inch(es), **k** knit,
mm millimetres, **0** no stitches or times, **p** purl,
st(s) stitch(es), **tog** together.
K2tog insert the right hand needle through the
2nd and 1st stitches on the left hand needle
and knit them together to form a single stitch.
P2tog insert the right hand needle purlways
through the 1st and 2nd stitches on the left
hand needle and purl them together to form a
single stitch.
Rib2tog if the next stitch is to be knit then
k2tog, if it is to be purl then p2tog.
M1 make 1 stitch – pick up loop between last
and next stitch and knit into the back of this
loop (this will now be referred to as m1).
S1p slip 1 stitch purlways with yarn at back –
insert the right hand needle into next stitch as if
to purl but just slip it off the left hand needle
onto the right hand needle without working.
S2p slip 2 stitches purlways with yarn at back
– insert the right hand needle into next stitch as
if to purl but just slip it off the left hand needle
onto the right hand needle without working.
C8B slip next 4 sts to back on CN, k4 then k4
from CN.

T6B slip next 2 sts to back on CN, k4 then k2
from CN.
T6F slip next 4 sts to front on CN, k2 then k4
from CN.
T6BP slip next 2 sts to back on CN, k4 then
p1, k1 from CN.
T6FP slip next 4 sts to front on CN, k1, p1
then k4 from CN.
C6BP slip next 2 sts to back on CN, k4 then
p2, from CN.
C6B slip next 3 sts to back on CN, k3 then k3
from CN.
C6FP slip next 4 sts to front on CN, p2 then
k4 from CN.
T5B slip next st to back on CN, k4 then p1
from CN.
T5BB slip next 2 sts to back on CN, k3 then
k2 from CN.
T5FF slip next 3 sts to front on CN, k2 then
k3 from CN.
T5F slip next 4 sts to front on CN, p1 then k4
from CN.
T4B slip next st to back on CN, k3 then k1
from CN.
T4F slip next 3 sts to front on CN, k1 then k3
from CN.

T4FB slip next 3 sts to front on CN, p1 then k3 from CN.

T4BB slip next st to back on CN, k3 then p1 from CN.

T5FB slip next 3 sts to front on CN, p2 then k3 from CN.

T5BP slip next 2 sts to back on CN, k3 then p2 from CN.

Circle the size you wish to make

FRONT

Regularly measure the width of the front as you knit. The Front should measure approximately 26 [28:31]cm, (10¼ [11:12]in) across.

Using your smaller needles cast on 62 [72:72] sts.

1st Row. (this will be the right side of the work - **rs**) K1, s1p, k3, * s2p, k3, repeat from * to last 2 sts, s1p, k1.

2nd Row. P2, * k3, p2, repeat from * to end. These 2 rows form 3x2 rib.

Work 5 rows.

8th Row. Rib 30 [35:35], rib2tog, rib 30 [35:35]. You will now have 61 [71:71] sts on the needle.

Change to your larger needles and proceed as follows:-

Next Row. K14 [7:19], k2tog, (k4, k2tog) 1 [3:1] times, k6 [6:5], m1, (k1, m1) 2 [2:3] times, increase in next st, m1, (k1, m1) 2 [2:3] times, k6 [6:5], k2tog, (k4, k2tog) 1 [3:1] times, k14 [7:19].

You will now have 64 [70:76] sts on the needle.

For 2nd size only
Next Row. K31, p8, k31.
Next Row. P31, k8, p31.

For 3rd size only
Next Row. K34, p8, k34.
1st Row. P34, C8B, p34.

2nd Row. K34, p8, k34.
3rd Row. P34, k8, p34.
4th Row. K34, p8, k34.
Repeat 3rd and 4th rows once.
7th Row. P34, k8, p34.

For all 3 sizes
Next Row. K28 [31:34], p8, k28 [31:34].
1st Row. P28 [31:34], C8B, p28 [31:34].
2nd Row. K28 [31:34], p8, k28 [31:34].
3rd Row. P28 [31:34], k8, p28 [31:34].
4th Row. K28 [31:34], p8, k28 [31:34].
Repeat 3rd and 4th rows twice.
9th Row. P28 [31:34], C8B, p28 [31:34].
10th Row. As 4th row.
11th Row. P26 [29:32], T6B, T6F, p26 [29:32].
12th Row. K26 [29:32], p12, k26 [29:32].
13th Row. P24 [27:30], T6BP, k4, T6FP, p24 [27:30].
14th Row. K24 [27:30], p4, k1, p6, k1, p4, k24 [27:30].
15th Row. P22 [25:28], C6BP, p1, C6B, p1, C6FP, p22 [25:28].
16th Row. K22 [25:28], p4, k3, p6, k3, p4, k22 [25:28].
17th Row. P20 [23:26], C6BP, p3, k6, p3, C6FP, p20 [23:26].
18th Row. K20 [23:26], p4, k5, p6, k5, p4, k20 [23:26].
19th Row. P18 [21:24], C6BP, p5, k6, p5, C6FP, p18 [21:24].
20th Row. K18 [21:24], p4, k7, p6, k7, p4, k18 [21:24].
21st Row. P16 [19:22], C6BP, p7, C6B, p7, C6FP, p16 [19:22].
22nd Row. K16 [19:22], p4, k9, p6, k9, p4, k16 [19:22].
23rd Row. P15 [18:21], T5B, p7, T5BB, T5FF, p7, T5F, p15 [18:21].
24th Row. K15 [18:21], p4, k8, p3, k4, p3, k8, p4, k15 [18:21].
25th Row. P14 [17:20], T5B, p7, T4B, k4, T4F, p7, T5F, p14 [17:20].
26th Row. K14 [17:20], p4, k8, p3, k6, p3, k8, p4, k14 [17:20].
27th Row. P13 [16:19], T5B, p7, T4B, k6,

T4F, p7, T5F, p13 [16:19].
28th Row. K13 [16:19], p4, k8, p3, k8, p3, k8, p4, k13 [16:19].
29th Row. P12 [15:18], T5B, p7, T4B, k8, T4F, p7, T5F, p12 [15:18].
30th Row. K12 [15:18], p4, k8, p3, k10, p3, k8, p4, k12 [15:18].
31st Row. P12 [15:18], T5F, p7, T4FB, k8, T4BB, p7, T5B, p12 [15:18].
32nd Row. K13 [16:19], p4, k8, p3, k8, p3, k8, p4, k13 [16:19].
33rd Row. P13 [16:19], T5F, p7, T4FB, k6, T4BB, p7, T5B, p13 [16:19].
34th Row. K14 [17:20], p4, k8, p3, k6, p3, k8, p4, k14 [17:20].
35th Row. P14 [17:20], T5F, p7, T4FB, k4, T4BB, p7, T5B, p14 [17:20].
36th Row. K15 [18:21], p4, k8, p3, k4, p3, k8, p4, k15 [18:21].
37th Row. P15 [18:21], T5F, p7, T5FB, T5BP, p7, T5B, p15 [18:21].
38th Row. K16 [19:22], p4, k9, p6, k9, p4, k16 [19:22].
39th Row. P16 [19:22], C6FP, p7, C6B, p7, C6BP, p16 [19:22].
40th Row. K18 [21:24], p4, k7, p6, k7, p4, k18 [21:24].
41st Row. P18 [21:24], C6FP, p5, k6, p5, C6BP, p18 [21:24].
42nd Row. K20 [23:26], p4, k5, p6, k5, p4, k20 [23:26].
43rd Row. P20 [23:26], C6FP, p3, k6, p3, C6BP, p20 [23:26].
44th Row. K22 [25:28], p4, k3, p6, k3, p4, k22 [25:28].
45th Row. P22 [25:28], C6FP, p1, C6B, p1, C6BP, p22 [25:28].
46th Row. K24 [27:30], p4, k1, p6, k1, p4, k24 [27:30].
47th Row. P24 [27:30], C6FP, k4, C6BP, p24 [27:30].
48th Row. K26 [29:32], p12, k26 [29:32].
49th Row. P26 [29:32], C6FP, C6BP, p26 [29:32].
50th Row. K28 [31:34], p8, k28 [31:34].
51st Row. P28 [31:34], C8B, p28 [31:34].

52nd Row. K28 [31:34], p8, k28 [31:34].
53rd Row. P28 [31:34], k8, p28 [31:34].
54th Row. K28 [31:34], p8, k28 [31:34].
Repeat 53rd and 54th rows twice.
59th Row. P28 [31:34], C8B, p28 [31:34].
60th Row. K28 [31:34], p8, k28 [31:34].

For 1st size only
The Front should measure approximately 24cm, (9½in), in length at this point. (If knitted at the correct row tension there should be 62 rows in pattern after 8 rib rows).

For 2nd size only
61st Row. P31, k8, p31.
62nd Row. K31, p8, k31.
The Front should measure approximately [26]cm, (10¼in), in length at this point (if knitted at the correct row tension there should be [66] rows in pattern after 8 rib rows).

For 3rd size only
61st Row. P34, k8, p34.
62nd Row. K34, p8, k34.
Rep 61st and 62nd rows twice.
67th Row. P34, C8B, p34.
68th Row. K34, p8, k34.
69th Row. P34, k8, p34.
70th Row. K34, p8, k34.
The Front should measure approximately [31]cm, (12in), in length at this point. (If knitted at the correct row tension there should be [80] rows in pattern after 8 rib rows).

For all 3 sizes
** Shape Neck
Beginning with the right side of the work facing you, divide for the neck as follows:-
P23 [26:29], turn, slip remaining 41 [44:47] sts

onto a stitch holder. You will come back to these
41 [44:47] sts later to work the second side of neck.

Next Row. Knit.
Work 2 rows decrease 1 st at neck edge in every row. You will now have 21 [24:27] sts on the needle.
Work 5 [5:3] rows decrease 1 st at neck edge in 1st and every following alternate row.
You will now have 18 [21:25] sts on the needle.

For 2nd and 3rd sizes only
Work [4:8] rows decrease 1 st at neck edge in every following 4th row. You will now have [20:23] sts on the needle.

For all 3 sizes
Work 4 rows straight.

Shoulder Edging
Change to your smaller needles and proceed as follows:-
Next Row. K4 [4:2], m1, (k2 [4:5], m1) 5 [3:4] times, k4 [4:1].
You will now have 24 [24:28] sts on the needle.
1st Row. P1, * k2, p2, repeat from * to last 3 sts, k2, p1.
2nd Row. K1, p2, * k2, p2, repeat from * to last st, k1.
3rd Row. Rib 7 [7:8], cast off 2 sts, rib 6 [6:8], cast off 2 sts, rib 5 [5:6].
4th Row. Rib 6 [6:7], cast on 2 sts, rib 7 [7:9], cast on 2 sts, rib 7 [7:8].
Work 1 row in rib.
Cast off in rib.
To work the second side of the neck return the 41 [44:47] sts left on a stitch holder onto the main needle.
With right side of work facing you, slip 18 sts onto a stitch holder, rejoin yarn and purl to

end.
You will now have 23 [26:29] sts on the needle.
Next Row. Knit.
Work 2 rows decrease 1 st at neck edge in every row. You will now have 21 [24:27] sts on the needle.
Work 5 [5:3] rows decrease 1 st at neck edge in 1st and every following alternate row.
You will now have 18 [21:25] sts on the needle.

For 2nd and 3rd sizes only
Work [4:8] rows decrease 1 st at neck edge in every following 4th row. You will now have [20:23] sts on the needle.
For all 3 sizes
Work 5 rows straight.
Cast off.

BACK
Using your smaller needles cast on 62 [72:72] sts.
Work 8 rows in 3x2 rib.
Next Row. (decrease row) K5 [8:8] k2tog, (k8 [4:16], k2tog) 5 [9:3] times, k5 [8:8]. You will now have 56 [62:68] sts on the needle.
Change to your larger needles and proceed as follows:-
Next Row. Knit.

Reversed stocking stitch
1st Row. Purl.
2nd Row. Knit.
These 2 rows form reversed stocking stitch.
Work in reversed stocking stitch for the remainder of the back as follows:-
Continue until back measures same as front to **.
Work 6 [6:8] rows straight.

Shape Neck
Beginning with the right side of the work facing you, divide for the neck as follows:-
P20 [23:26], turn, slip remaining 36 [39:42] sts onto a stitch holder. You will come back to

these 36 [39:42] sts later to work the second side of neck.

For 1st size only

Work 2 rows decrease 1 st at neck edge in every row. You will now have 18 sts on the needle.

For 2nd and 3rd sizes only

Next Row. Knit.
Work 5 rows decrease 1 st at neck edge in 1st and every following alternate row. You will now have [20:23] sts on the needle.

For all 3 sizes

Work 5 rows straight.
Cast off.
To work the second side of the neck return the 36 [39:42] sts left on a stitch holder onto the main needle.
With right side of work facing you, slip 16 sts onto a stitch holder, rejoin yarn and purl to end.
You will now have 20 [23:26] sts on the needle.

For 1st size only

Work 2 rows decrease 1 st at neck edge in every row. You will now have 18 sts on the needle.

For 2nd and 3rd sizes only

Next Row. Knit.
Work 5 rows decrease 1 st at neck edge in 1st and every following alternate row. You will now have [20:23] sts on the needle.

For all 3 sizes

Work 4 rows straight.

Shoulder shaping

Change to your smaller needles and proceed as follows:-

Next Row. K4 [4:2], m1, (k2 [4:5], m1) 5 [3:4] times, k4 [4:1]. You will now have 24 [24:28] sts on the needle.
1st Row. P1, * k2, p2, repeat from * to last 3 sts, k2, p1.
2nd Row. K1, p2, * k2, p2, repeat from * to last st, k1.
Work 3 rows in rib.
Cast off in rib.

SLEEVES (Both alike)

Using your smaller needles cast on 39 [39:43] sts.
1st Row. K1 [1:3], * s2p, k3, repeat from * to last 3 [3:0] sts, (s2p, k1) 1 [1:0] times.
2nd Row. K1 [1:0], p2 [2:0], * k3, p2, repeat from * to last 1 [1:3] sts, k1 [1:3].
These 2 rows form rib.
Work 6 rows in rib.
Next Row. Knit to end decrease 3 [1:3] sts evenly across row. You will now have 36 [38:40] sts on the needle.
Change to your larger needles and knit 1 row.
Beginning with a purl row work in reversed stocking stitch for the remainder of the sleeve as follows:-
Work 9 [17:9] rows increasing 1 st at each end of 1st and every following 8th row (there will be 7 rows straight between each increase row). You will now have 40 [44:44] sts on the needle.
Work 20 [20:40] rows increasing 1 st at each end of 10th and every following 10th row (there will be 9 rows straight between each increase row). You will now have 44 [48:52] sts on the needle.
Work without further shaping until sleeve is 17 [20:24]cm, (6½ [8:9½]in), or length required, finishing after a knit row.

Shape Sleeve Top

Cast off 3 sts at beginning of each of the next

10 [14:10] rows. You will now have 14 [6:22] sts on the needle.

For 1st and 3rd sizes only

Cast off 4 sts at beginning of each of the next 2 [4] rows. You will now have 6 sts on the needle.

For all 3 sizes

Cast off remaining 6 sts.

NECKBAND

Join right shoulder seam. With right side of work facing you, using your smaller needles pick up and knit 5 sts evenly down shoulder edging, 12 [16:17] sts evenly down left side of neck, work across 18 sts left on a stitch holder at front neck as follows:- k2tog, k2, k2tog, k6, k2tog, k2, k2tog, pick up and knit 10 [14:15] sts evenly up right side of neck, 8 [10:11] sts evenly down right side of back neck, knit across 16 sts left on a stitch holder at back of neck, pick up and knit 4 [6:7] sts evenly up left side of back neck and 5 sts evenly up shoulder edging. 74 [86:90] sts.
1st Row. * P2, k2, repeat from * to last 2 sts, p2.
2nd Row. K2, * p2, k2, repeat from * to end.
These 2 rows form 2x2 rib.
Next Row. Rib to last 5 sts, cast off 2 sts, rib 2.
Next Row. Rib 3, cast on 2 sts, rib to end.
Work 1 row in rib.
Cast off in rib.

TO MAKE UP

Fold sleeves in half lengthways then placing folds to shoulder seams, sew sleeves in position for approximately 11 [12:13]cm, (4¼ [4¾:5¼]in), from top of shoulders. Join side and sleeve seams. Sew on buttons. Pin out garment to the measurement given and cover with damp cloths until dry (refer to page 2). See ball band for washing and further care instructions.

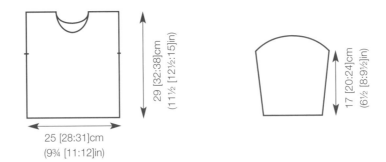

29 [32:38]cm
(11½ [12½:15]in)

25 [28:31]cm
(9¾ [11:12]in)

17 [20:24]cm
(6½ [8:9½]in)

Little Anchor Man, Blue Anchor Man, Big Anchor Man and Little Anchor Beanies

worked in Sublime baby cashmere merino silk dk

You will also need
1 pair of 4mm (UK8 – USA6) Knitting Needles for the main knitting (or the size required to give the correct tension).
1 pair of 3¼mm (UK10 – USA3) Knitting Needles for the edgings (or a needle 2 sizes smaller than you use for the main knitting). Stitch holders and 3 Buttons each for Little Anchor Man, Blue Anchor Man and Big Anchor Man.

TENSION
Please take a little time now to knit a stocking stitch tension square. **Using 4mm needles cast**

Sizes Age	0-6 months	6-12 months	1-2 years	2-3 years	

Little Anchor Beanies to fit an average size baby's/child's head for the age indicated.

Little Anchor Man and Blue Anchor Man

	0-6 months	6-12 months	1-2 years	2-3 years	
To Fit Chest	41	46	51	56	cm
	16	18	20	22	in
Actual Size	46	51	56	61	cm
	18	20	22	24	in
Full Length (approximately)	24	28	32	38	cm
	9½	11	12½	15	in
Sleeve Length (approximately)	15	17	20	24	cm
	6	6½	8	9½	in

Big Anchor Man

	0-6 months	6-12 months	1-2 years	2-3 years	
To Fit Chest		46	51	56	cm
		18	20	22	in
Actual Size		51	56	61	cm
		20	22	24	in
Full Length (approximately)		28	32	38	cm
		11	12½	15	in
Sleeve Length (approximately)		17	20	24	cm
		6½	8	9½	in

MATERIALS

	0-6 months	6-12 months	1-2 years	2-3 years	
Little Anchor Man					
K001 Sublime baby cashmere merino silk dk shade 03 vanilla for main	2	3	4	4	50g balls
K001 Sublime baby cashmere merino silk dk shade 51 button for contrast	1	1	1	1	50g balls
Blue Anchor Man					
K001 Sublime baby cashmere merino silk dk shade 125 bathtub	3	3	4	5	50g balls
Big Anchor Man					
K001 Sublime baby cashmere merino silk dk shade 123 sleepy		3	4	5	50g balls
Little Anchor Beanie (2 colours)					
K001 Sublime baby cashmere merino silk dk shade 03 vanilla for main	1	1	1	1	50g balls
K001 Sublime baby cashmere merino silk dk shade 51 button for contrast	1	1	1	1	50g balls
Little Anchor Beanie (1 colour)					
K001 Sublime baby cashmere merino silk dk shade 125 bathtub	1	1	1	1	50g balls

on 22 stitches and work 28 rows in stocking stitch (1 row knit, 1 row purl). This should now measure 10cm, (4in) square. If your square isn't the correct width please refer to page 2.

ABBREVIATIONS

cm centimetres, **dk** double knitting, **g** grammes, **in** inch(es), **inc** increase(ing), **k** knit, **mm** millimetres, **0** no stitches, times or rows, **patt** pattern, **p** purl, **rep** repeat, **st(s)** stitch(es), **tog** together, **ws** wrong side.

K2tog insert the right hand needle through the 2nd and 1st stitches on the left hand needle and knit them together to form a single stitch.

P2tog insert the right hand needle purlways through the 1st and 2nd stitches on the left hand needle and purl them together to form a single stitch.

Yfwd bring yarn to front between needles then take the yarn over the top of the right hand needle to form a single stitch.

Circle the size you wish to make

LITTLE ANCHOR MAN
BACK

Regularly measure the width of the back as you knit. The Back should measure approximately 23 [26:28:30]cm, (9 [10¼: 11:11¾]in) across.

Using your smaller needles and contrast yarn cast on 51 [57:61:67] sts.

1st Row (this will be the right side of the work – **rs**). Using main yarn, knit.
This row forms garter stitch.
Working in garter stitch work 1 row in main yarn, 2 rows in contrast yarn, 2 rows in main yarn and 2 rows in contrast yarn.
Change to your main needles and main yarn, work the remainder of the back as follows:-

Pattern
1st Row. Knit.
2nd Row. Purl.

3rd Row. K9 [12:6:9], * p1, k15, rep from * to last 10 [13:7:10] sts, p1, k9 [12:6:9].
4th Row. P8 [11:5:8], k3, * p13, k3, rep from * to last 8 [11:5:8] sts, p8 [11:5:8].
5th Row. K7 [10:4:7], * p1, k3, p1, k11, rep from * to last 12 [15:9:12] sts, p1, k3, p1, k7 [10:4:7].
6th Row. P6 [9:3:6], (k1, p2) twice, k1, * p9, (k1, p2) twice, k1, rep from * to last 6 [9:3:6] sts, p6 [9:3:6].
7th Row. Knit.
8th Row. As 6th row.
9th Row. Knit.
10th Row. P9 [12:6:9], k1, * p15, k1, rep from * to last 9 [12:6:9] sts, p9 [12:6:9]
11th Row. Knit.
12th Row. As 10th row.
13th Row. K7 [10:4:7], * p5, k11, rep from * to last 12 [15:9:12] sts, p5, k7 [10:4:7].
14th Row. As 10th row.
15th Row. K8 [11:5:8], * p1, k1, p1, k13, rep from * to last 11 [14:8:11] sts, p1, k1, p1, k8 [11:5:8].
16th Row. As 10th row.
17th Row. Knit.
18th Row. Purl.
19th Row. K17 [4:14:17], * p1, k15, rep from * to last 2 [5:15:2] sts, p0 [1:1:0], k2 [4:14:2].
20th Row. P3 [3:0:3], k0 [3:0:0], * p13, k3, rep from * to last 16 [3:13:16] sts, p16 [3: 13:16].
21st Row. K15 [2:12:15], * p1, k3, p1, k11, rep from * to last 4 [7:1:4] sts, (p1, k3, p1) 0 [1:0:0] times, k4 [2:1:4].
22nd Row. P5 [1:2:5], (k1, p2, k1, p2, k1) 0 [1:0:0] times, * p9, (k1, p2) twice, k1, rep from * to last 14 [1:11:14] sts, p14 [1:11:14].
23rd Row. Knit.
24th Row. As 22nd row.
25th Row. Knit.
26th Row. P2 [4:14:2], k0 [1:1:0], * p15, k1, rep from * to last 17 [4:14:17] sts, p17 [4: 14:17].
27th Row. Knit.
28th Row. As 26th row.
29th Row. K15 [2:12:15], * p5, k11, rep from

* to last 4 [7:1:4] sts, p0 [5:0:0], k4 [2:1:4].
30th Row. As 26th row.
31st Row. K16 [3:13:16], * p1, k1, p1, k13, rep from * to last 3 [6:0:3] sts, (p1, k1, p1) 0 [1:0:0] times, k3 [3:0:3].
32nd Row. P2 [4:14:2], k0 [1:1:0], * p15, k1, rep from * to last 17 [4:14:17] sts, p17 [4: 14:17].
These 32 rows form anchor patt.
Repeat them until back measures 20 [24: 28:34]cm, (8 [9½:11:13½]in), finishing after a ws row.

Neck Shaping

Beginning with the right side of the work facing you, divide for the neck as follows:- Patt 21 [23:23:26], turn, slip remaining 30 [34: 38:41] sts onto a stitch holder. You will come back to these 30 [34:38:41] sts later to work the second side of neck. Patt to end. Work a further 4 rows decreasing 1 st at neck edge in every row. You will now have 17 [19:19:22] sts on the needle. Work 4 [4:4:6] rows straight. Cast off in patt.
To work the second side of the neck return the 30 [34:38:41] sts left on a stitch holder onto the main needle. With the right side of the work facing you, slip first 9 [11:15:15] sts onto a stitch holder and leave at centre back of the neck. You will come back to these 9 [11: 15:15] sts later for neck edging. Rejoin main yarn to the remaining 21 [23:23:26] sts and patt to end. Patt 1 row back then work a further 4 rows decreasing 1 st at neck edge in every row. You will now have 17 [19:19:22] sts on the needle.
Work 2 [2:2:4] rows straight.

Shoulder Edging

Change to your smaller needles and working in garter stitch work 2 rows in contrast yarn, 2 rows in main yarn and 1 row in contrast yarn. Using contrast yarn cast off knitways.

FRONT

Work the front as given for Back until front is

6 rows less than Back to neck shaping.

Neck Shaping

Beginning with the right side of the work facing you, divide for the neck as follows:- Patt 22 [24:24:27], turn, slip remaining 29 [33: 37:40] sts onto a stitch holder. You will come back to these 29 [33:37:40] sts later to work the second side of neck. Patt 1 row back then work 2 rows decreasing 1 st at neck edge in every row. You will now have 20 [22:22:25] sts on the needle. Work a further 5 rows decreasing 1 st at neck edge in 1st, 3rd and 5th rows. You will now have 17 [19:19:22] sts on the needle.

Work 5 [5:5:7] rows straight.

Shoulder Edging

Change to your smaller needles and working in garter stitch work 2 rows in contrast yarn.

Next Row. Using main yarn, k5 [5:5:6], yfwd, k2tog, k4 [6:6:7], yfwd, k2tog, k4 [4:4:5]. Work 1 row in main yarn and 1 row in contrast yarn.

Using contrast yarn cast off knitways.

To work the second side of the neck return the 29 [33:37:40] sts left on a stitch holder onto the main needle. With right side of the work facing you, slip first 7 [9:13:13] sts onto a stitch holder and leave at centre front of the neck. You will come back to these 7 [9:13:13] sts later for neck edging. Rejoin main yarn to the remaining 22 [24:24:27] sts and patt to end. Patt 1 row back then work 2 rows decreasing 1 st at neck edge in every row. You will now have 20 [22:22:25] sts on the needle. Work a further 5 rows decreasing 1 st at neck edge in 1st, 3rd and 5th rows. You will now have 17 [19:19:22] sts on the needle.

Work 7 [7:7:9] rows straight.

Cast off in patt.

SLEEVES (Both alike)

Using your smaller needles and contrast yarn cast on 35 [35:37:39] sts.

1st Row. (this will be the right side of the work – rs) Using main yarn, knit.

Working in garter stitch work 1 row in main yarn, 2 rows in contrast yarn, 2 rows in main yarn and 1 row in contrast yarn.

8th Row. Using contrast yarn, knit to end decreasing 2 sts evenly across row. You will now have 33 [33:35:37] sts on the needle. Change to your main needles and main yarn work the remainder of the sleeve as follows:-

Pattern

1st Row. Knit

2nd Row. Purl.

3rd Row. Inc in 1st st, k7 [7:8:9], p1, k15, p1, k6 [6:7:8], inc in next st, k1. You will now have 35 [35:37:39] sts on the needle.

4th Row. P8 [8:9:10], k3, p13, k3, p8 [8:9:10].

5th Row. K7 [7:8:9], p1, k3, p1, k11, p1, k3, p1, k7 [7:8:9].

6th Row. P6 [6:7:8], (k1, p2) twice, k1, p9, (k1, p2) twice, k1, p6 [6:7:8].

7th Row. Knit.

8th Row. P6 [6:7:8], (k1, p2) twice, k1, p9, (k1, p2) twice, k1, p6 [6:7:8].

9th Row. (Inc in 1st st) 0 [0:1:1] times, knit to last 0 [0:2:2] sts, (inc in next st, k1) 0 [0:1:1] times. You will now have 35 [35:39:41] sts on the needle.

10th Row. P9 [9:11:12], K1, P15, k1, p9 [9: 11:12].

11th Row. (Inc in 1st st) 0 [1:0:0] times, knit to last 0 [2:0:0] sts, (inc in next st, k1) 0 [1:0:0] times. You will now have 35 [37:39:41] sts on the needle.

12th Row. P9 [10:11:12], k1, p15, k1, p9 [10: 11:12].

13th Row. K7 [8:9:10], p5, k11, p5, k7 [8: 9:10].

14th Row. P9 [10:11:12], k1, p15, k1, p9 [10: 11:12].

15th Row. (Inc in 1st st) 1 [0:1:1] times, k7 [9: 9:10], p1, k1, p1, k13, p1, k1, p1, k6 [9:8:9], (inc in next st, k1) 1 [0:1:1] times. You will now have 37 [37:41:43] sts on the needle.

16th Row. P10 [10:12:13], k1, p15, k1, p10 [10:12:13].

17th Row. Knit.

18th Row. Purl.

19th Row. (Inc in 1st st) 0 [1:0:0] times, k2 [1: 4:5], (p1, k15) twice, p1, k2 [0:4:5], (inc in next st, k1) 0 [1:0:0] times. You will now have 37 [39:41:43] sts on the needle.

20th Row. P1 [2:3:4], k3, (p13, k3) twice, p1 [2:3:4].

21st Row. (Inc in 1st st) 0 [0:1:1] times, k0 [1: 1:2], (p1, k3, p1, k11) twice, p1, k3, p1, k0 [1: 0:1], (inc in next st, k1) 0 [0:1:1] times. You will now have 37 [39:43:45] sts on the needle.

22nd Row. P0 [0:2:3], k0 [1:1:1], (p2, k1) twice, p9, (k1, p2) twice, k1, p9, (k1, p2) twice, k0 [1:1:1], p0 [0:2:3].

23rd Row. Knit.

24th Row. As 22nd row.

25th Row. Knit.

26th Row. P2 [3:5:6], k1, (p15, k1) twice, p2 [3:5:6].

27th Row. (Inc in 1st st) 0 [1:1:0] times, knit to last 0 [2:2:0] sts, (inc in next st, k1) 0 [1:1:0] times. You will now have 37 [41:45:45] sts on the needle.

28th Row. P2 [4:6:6], k1, (p15, k1) twice, p2 [4:6:6].

29th Row. (Inc in 1st st) 1 [0:0:1] times, k0 [2: 4:3], p4 [5:5:5], k11, p5, k11, p3 [5:5:5], k0 [2: 4:2] (inc in next st) 1 [0:0:1] times, p1 [0:0:0], k0 [0:0:1]. You will now have 39 [41:45:47] sts on the needle.

30th Row. P3 [4:6:7], k1, (p15, k1) twice, p3 [4:6:7].

31st Row. K2 [3:5:6], (p1, k1, p1, k13) twice, p1, k1, p1, k2 [3:5:6].

32nd Row. P3 [4:6:7], k1, (p15, k1) twice, p3 [4:6:7].

These 32 rows set position for anchor patt. Work in anchor patt for the remainder of the sleeve as follows:-

For 2nd, 3rd and 4th sizes only

Work [3:9:21] rows inc 1 st at each end of [3rd:1st:5th] and every following [0:8th:8th] row (there will be [0:7:7] rows straight between each increase row), inc sts should be worked in patt. You will now have [43:49:53] sts on the needle

For all 4 sizes

Work without further shaping until the sleeve is 15 [17:20:24]cm, (6 [6½:8:9½]in), finishing after a ws row.

Shape Sleeve Top

Cast off 3 sts in patt at beginning of each of the next 12 [10:12:16] rows. You will now have 3 [13:13:5] sts on the needle.

For 2nd and 3rd sizes only

Cast off 4 sts in patt at beginning of each of the next 2 rows. You will now have [5:5] sts on the needle.

For all 4 sizes

Cast off remaining 3 [5:5:5] sts in patt.

NECK EDGING

Join the right shoulder seam then using your smaller needles and contrast yarn pick up and knit sts around neck shaping as follows:-
With rs of the work facing you, pick up and knit 4 sts evenly down side edge of shoulder edging, 10 [10:10:12] sts evenly down left side of front neck, knit across 7 [9:13:13] sts left on a stitch holder at centre front neck, 14 [14:14:16] sts evenly up right side of front neck, 8 [8:8:10] sts evenly down right side of back neck, knit across 9 [11:15:15] sts left on a stitch holder at centre back neck, 5 [5:5:7] sts evenly up left side of back neck and 4 sts evenly up side edge of shoulder edging. You will now have 61 [65:73:81] sts on the needle.
Working in garter stitch work 1 row in contrast yarn.
Next Row. Using main yarn, k2, yfwd, k2tog, knit to end.
Work 1 row in main yarn and 1 row in contrast yarn.
Using contrast yarn, cast off knitways.

TO MAKE UP

Placing left front shoulder edging over left back shoulder edging join together at side edge. Fold sleeves in half lengthways, then placing folds to shoulder seams, sew sleeves in position for approximately 10 [11:12:13]cm, (4 [4¼:4¾:5¼]in) from top of shoulder. Join side and sleeve seams. Sew on buttons. Pin out garment to the measurement given and cover with damp cloths until dry (refer to page 2). See ball band for washing and further care instructions.

BLUE ANCHOR MAN

Work as given for Little Anchor Man using one colour only.

BIG ANCHOR MAN
FRONT

Regularly measure the width of the back as you knit (see measurement chart).
For 2nd, 3rd and 4th sizes only
Using your smaller needles cast on [57:61:67] sts.
1st Row (this will be the right side of the work – **rs**) knit.
This row forms garter stitch.
Work 7 rows in garter stitch. **

Change to your main needles and work [4:10:18] rows in stocking stitch.

Pattern

1st Row. Knit.
2nd Row. P[28:30:33], k1, p[28:30:33].
3rd Row. Knit.
4th Row. P[27:29:32], k3, p[27:29:32].
5th Row. Knit.
6th Row. P[25:27:30], k7, p[25:27:30].
7th Row. Knit.
8th Row. P[22:24:27], k13, p[22:24:27].
9th Row. Knit.
10th Row. P[20:22:25], k5, p2, k3, p2, k5, p[20:22:25].
11th Row. Knit.
12th Row. P[18:20:23], k5, p4, k3, p4, k5, p[18:20:23].
13th Row. Knit.
14th Row. P[16:18:21], k4, p7, k3, p7, k4, p[16:18:21].
15th Row. Knit.
16th Row. P[17:19:22], (k3, p7) twice, k3, p[17:19:22].
17th Row. Knit.
18th Row. P[19:21:24], k1, p7, k3, p7, k1, p[19:21:24].
19th Row. Knit.
20th Row. P[27:29:32], k3, p[27:29:32].
21st to 36th Row. Rep 19th and 20th rows 8 times.
37th Row. Knit.
38th Row. P[19:21:24], k19, p[19:21:24].
39th and 40th Rows. As 37th and 38th rows.
41st Row. Knit.
42nd Row. P[26:28:31], k5, p[26:28:31].
43rd Row. Knit.
44th Row. P[25:27:30], k2, p3, k2, p[25:27:30].
45th Row. Knit.
46th Row. P[25:27:30], k3, p1, k3, p[25:27:30].
47th Row. Knit.
48th Row. P[27:29:32], k3, p[27:29:32].
Beginning with a knit row work in stocking stitch for the remainder of the front as follows:-
Work [4:10:16] rows straight.

Neck Shaping

Beginning with the right side of the work facing you, divide for the neck as follows:- Knit [24:24:27], turn, slip remaining [33:37:40] sts onto a stitch holder. You will come back to these [33:37:40] sts later to work the second side of neck. Purl 1 row back then work 2 rows decreasing 1 st at neck edge in every row. You will now have [22:22:25] sts on the needle. Work a further 5 rows decreasing 1 st at neck edge in 1st, 3rd and 5th rows. You will now have [19:19:22] sts on the needle. Work [5:5:7] rows straight.

Shoulder Edging

Change to your smaller needles and knit 2 rows.
Next Row. K[5:5:6], yfwd, k2tog, k[6:6:7],

yfwd, k2tog, k[4:4:5].
Knit 2 rows.
Cast off knitways.
To work the second side of the neck return the [33:37:40] sts left on a stitch holder onto the main needle. With right side of the work facing you, slip first [9:13:13] sts onto a stitch holder and leave at centre front of the neck. You will come back to these [9:13:13] sts later for neck edging. Rejoin yarn to the remaining [24:24:27] sts and knit to end. Purl 1 row back then work 2 rows decreasing 1 st at neck edge in every row. You will now have [22:22:25] sts on the needle. Work a further 5 rows decreasing 1 st at neck edge in 1st, 3rd and 5th rows. You will now have [19:19:22] sts on the needle.
Work [7:7:9] rows straight.
Cast off.

BACK
Work the back as given for Front to **.
Change to your main needles and beginning with a knit row work in stocking stitch for the remainder of the back as follows:-
Work [62:74:88] rows straight.

Neck Shaping
Beginning with the right side of the work facing you, divide for the neck as follows:- Knit [23:23:26], turn, slip remaining [34:38:41] sts onto a stitch holder. You will come back to these [34:38:41] sts later to work the second side of neck. Purl 1 row back then work a further 4 rows decreasing 1 st at neck edge in every row. You will now have [19:19:22] sts on the needle. Work [4:4:6] rows without shaping. Cast off.
To work the second side of the neck return the [34:38:41] sts left on a stitch holder onto the main needle. With the right side of the work facing you, slip first [11:15:15] sts onto a stitch holder and leave at centre back of the neck. You will come back to these [11:15:15] sts later for neck edging. Rejoin yarn to the remaining [23:23:26] sts and knit to end. Purl 1 row back then work a further 4 rows

decreasing 1 st at neck edge in every row. You will now have [19:19:22] sts on the needle.
Work [2:2:4] rows straight.

Shoulder Edging
Change to your smaller needles and work 5 rows in garter stitch. Cast off knitways.

SLEEVES (Both alike)
Using your smaller needles cast on [35:37:39] sts and work 7 rows in garter stitch.
8th Row. Knit to end decreasing 2 sts evenly across row. [33:35:37] sts.
Change to your main needles and working in stocking stitch for the remainder of the sleeve as follows:-
Work [35:33:21] rows inc 1 st at each end of 3rd and every following [8th:6th:6th] row (there will be [7:5:5] rows straight between each increase row). You will now have [43:47:45] sts on the needle

For 3rd and 4th sizes only
Work [8:32] rows inc 1 st at each end of 8th and every following [0:8th] row (there will be 7 rows straight between each increase row). You will now have [49:53] sts on the needle.

For all 3 sizes
Work without further shaping until the sleeve is [17:20:24]cm, ([6½:8:9½]in), finishing after a ws row.

Shape Sleeve Top
Cast off 3 sts at beginning of each of the next [10:12:16] rows. You will now have [13:13:5] sts on the needle.

For 2nd and 3rd sizes only
Cast off 4 sts at beginning of each of the next 2 rows. You will now have [5:5] sts on the needle.

For all 3 sizes
Cast off remaining 5 sts.

NECK EDGING
Join the right shoulder seam then using your smaller needles and yarn pick up and knit sts around neck shaping as follows:-

With rs of the work facing you, pick up and knit 4 sts evenly down side edge of shoulder edging, [10:10:12] sts evenly down left side of front neck, knit across [9:13:13] sts left on a stitch holder at centre front neck, [14:14:16] sts evenly up right side of front neck, [8:8:10] sts evenly down right side of back neck, knit across [11:15:15] sts left on a stitch holder at centre back neck, [5:5:7] sts evenly up left side of back neck and 4 sts evenly up side edge of shoulder edging. You will now have [65:73:81] sts on the needle.
Knit 1 row.
Next Row. K2, yfwd, k2tog, knit to end.
Knit 2 rows.
Cast off knitways.

TO MAKE UP
Placing left front shoulder edging over left back shoulder edging join together at side edge. Fold sleeves in half lengthways, then placing folds to shoulder seams, sew sleeves in position for approximately [11:12:13]cm, ([4¼:4¾:5¼]in) from top of shoulder. Join side and sleeve seams. Sew on buttons. Pin out garment to the measurement given and cover with damp cloths until dry (refer to page 2). See ball band for washing and further care instructions.

LITTLE ANCHOR BEANIE (2 colours)
Using your smaller needles and contrast yarn cast on 75 [81:87:97] sts.
1st Row (this will be the right side of the work – **rs**). Using main yarn, knit.
This row forms garter stitch.
Working in garter stitch work 1 row in main yarn, 2 rows in contrast yarn, 2 rows in main yarn and 2 rows in contrast yarn.
Change to your main needles and main yarn, work 2 rows in stocking stitch.

Pattern

1st Row. Knit.

2nd Row. Purl.

3rd Row. K37 [40:43:48], p1, k37 [40:43:48].

4th Row. P36 [39:42:47], k3, p36 [39:42:47].

5th Row. K35 [38:41:46], p1, k3, p1, k35 [38:41:46].

6th Row. P34 [37:40:45], (k1, p2) twice, k1, p34 [37:40:45].

7th Row. K33 [36:39:44], p1, k7, p1, k33 [36:39:44].

8th Row. P37 [40:43:48], k1, p37 [40:43:48].

9th Row. As 7th row.

10th Row. As 8th row.

11th Row. Knit.

12th Row. As 8th row.

13th Row. Knit.

14th Row. As 8th row.

15th Row. K34 [37:40:45], p7, k34 [37:40:45].

16th Row. As 8th row.

17th Row. K36 [39:42:47], p1, k1, p1, k36 [39:42:47].

18th Row. P37 [40:43:48], k1, p37 [40:43:48].

Continue in stocking stitch until the beanie measures 11 [12:13:14]cm, (4¼ [4¾: 5¼:5½]in), finishing after a knit row.

Next Row. Purl to end inc 3 [0:0:2] sts evenly across row for 1st and 4th sizes only and decreasing 0 [3:2:0] sts evenly across row for 2nd and 3rd sizes only. You will now have 78 [78:85:99] sts on the needle.

Crown Shaping

1st Row. K1, (k2tog, k5) 11 [11:12:14] times. You will now have 67 [67:73:85] sts on the needle.

2nd and Every Alternate Row. Purl.

3rd Row. K1, (k2tog, k4) 11 [11:12:14] times. You will now have 56 [56:61:71] sts on the needle.

5th Row. K1, (k2tog, k3) 11 [11:12:14] times. You will now have 45 [45:49:57] sts on the needle.

7th Row. K1, (k2tog, k2) 11 [11:12:14] times.

You will now have 34 [34:37:43] sts on the needle.

9th Row. K1, (k2tog, k1) 11 [11:12:14] times. You will now have 23 [23:25:29] sts on the needle.

11th Row. K1, (k2tog) 11 [11:12:14] times. You will now have 12 [12:13:15] sts on the needle.

12th Row. (P2tog) 6 [6:6:7] times, p0 [0:1:1] You will now have 6 [6:7:8] sts on the needle.

Break off yarn, thread yarn through remaining 6 [6:7:8] sts, draw up and fasten off.

TO MAKE UP

Join back seam. Cover with a damp cloth until dry (refer to page 2). See ball band for washing and further care instructions.

LITTLE ANCHOR BEANIE (1 colour)

Work as given for Little Anchor Beanie with 2 colours using one colour only.

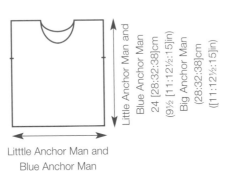

Litttle Anchor Man and
Blue Anchor Man
23 [26:28:31]cm
(9 [10¼:11:12]in)
Big Anchor Man
(26:28:31)cm
([10¼:11:12]in)

Little Anchor Man and Blue Anchor Man
24 [28:32:38]cm
(9½ [11:12½:15]in)
Big Anchor Man
(28:32:38)cm
([11:12½:15]in)

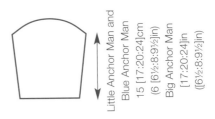

Little Anchor Man and Blue Anchor Man
15 [17:20:24]cm
(6 [6½:8:9½]in)
Big Anchor Man
[17:20:24]in
([6½:8:9½]in)

Sublime™

Ziggy Blanket

worked in Sublime baby
cashmere merino silk dk

You will also need
1 pair of 4mm (UK8 – USA6) Knitting
Needles for the main knitting (or the size
required to give the correct tension).
1 pair of 3¼mm (UK10 – USA3) Knitting
Needles for borders (or a needle 2 sizes
smaller than you use for the main knitting).

TENSION

Please take a little time now to knit a stocking
stitch tension square. **Using 4mm needles
cast on 22 stitches and work 28 rows in
stocking stitch (1 row knit, 1 row purl). This
should now measure 10cm, (4in) square.** If
your square isn't the correct width please refer
to page 2.
When worked at the correct tension the main
part of the blanket will measure approximately
108cm, (42½in), across.

ABBREVIATIONS

cm centimetres, **dk** double knitting,
g grammes, **in** inch(es), **mm** millimetres,
st(s) stitch(es), **k** knit, **p** purl.

MEASUREMENTS

Blanket (approximately)

108 x 108		cm
42½ x 42½		in

MATERIALS

K001 Sublime baby cashmere merino
silk dk shade 125 bathtub   13   50g balls

MAIN PART

Regularly measure the width of the blanket
as you knit. The Blanket should measure
approximately 100cm, (39½in) across.
Using your smaller needles cast on 221 sts.
1st Row. (this will be the right side of
work – **rs**) Knit.
This row forms garter stitch.
Repeat 1st row for 4cm, (1½in), finishing after a
wrong side row.
Change to your main needles and work in
pattern as follows:-

Pattern

1st Row. * P1, k19 repeat from * to last st, p1.
2nd Row. K1,* k1, p17, k2, repeat from * to
end.
3rd Row. * P3, k15, p2, repeat from * to last
st, p1
4th Row. K1,* k3, p13, k4, repeat from * to
end.
5th Row. P5, k11, p4, repeat from * to last
st, p1.
6th Row. K1, * k5, p9, k6, repeat from * to
end.
7th Row. * P7, k7, p6, repeat from * to last st,
p1.
8th Row. K1, * k7, p5, k8, repeat from * to
end.
9th Row. * P9, k3, p8, repeat from * to last st,
p1.
10th Row. K1, * k9, p1, k10, repeat from * to
end.
11th Row. * K1, p19, repeat from * to last st,
k1.
12th Row. P1, * p1, k17, p2, repeat from * to
end.
13th Row. * K3, p15, k2, repeat from * to last
st, k1.

14th Row. P1, * p3, k13, p4, repeat from * to
end.
15th Row. * K5, p11, k4, repeat from * to last
st, k1.
16th Row. P1, * p5, k9, p6, repeat from * to
end.
17th Row. * K7, p7, k6, repeat from * to last
st, k1.
18th Row. P1, * p7, k5, p8, repeat from * to
end.
19th Row. * K9, p3, k8, repeat from * to last
st, k1.
20th Row. P1, * p9, k1, p10, repeat from * to
end.
These 20 rows form pattern.
Repeat them until the work measures
approximately 104cm, (41in), finishing after a
10th or 20th row of pattern. Change to
smaller needles and work in garter stitch for
4cm, (1½in), finishing after a right side row.
Cast off knitways.

SIDE EDGINGS (Both alike)

With the right side of the work facing you and
using your smaller needles commencing at
cast on or cast off edge pick up and knit 9 sts
evenly along garter stitch edge of main part of
blanket, 221 sts evenly along side edge of
blanket and 9 sts evenly along garter stitch
edge. You will now have 239 sts on the
needle.
Work in garter stitch for 4cm, (1½in), finishing
after a right side row.
Cast off knitways.

TO COMPLETE

Pin out blanket to the measurement given and
cover with damp cloths until dry (refer to page
2). See ball band for washing and further care
instructions.

Sublime™

Little Petal Cardie and Peach Petal Cardie

worked in Sublime baby cashmere merino silk dk

You will also need
1 pair of 3¾mm (UK9 – USA5) Knitting Needles for the main knitting (or the size required to give the correct tension).
1 pair of 3¼mm (UK10 – USA3) Knitting Needles for the flowers (or a needle 2 sizes smaller than you use for the main knitting). Stitch Holders and 1 Button.

TENSION
Please take a little time now to knit a tension square. **Using 4mm needles cast on 22 stitches and work 28 rows in stocking stitch (1 row knit, 1 row purl). This should now measure 10cm, (4in) square.** If your square isn't the correct width please refer to page 2. As long as you knit the stocking stitch tension at the above tension 22 stitches and 44 rows

SIZES

Age	0–6 months	6–12 months	1–2 years	2–3 years	
To Fit Chest	41	46	51	56	cm
	16	18	20	22	in
Actual Size	45	50	55	61	cm
	17¾	19¾	21¾	24	in
Full Length	19	23	27	33	cm
	7½	9	10¾	13	in
Sleeve Length Little Petal	15	17	20	24	cm
	6	6½	8	9½	in
Peach Petal	1	1	1	1	cm
	½	½	½	½	in

MATERIALS
Little petal cardie

K001 Sublime baby cashmere merino silk dk in shade 05 waterlily	3	3	4	5	50g balls

Peach petal cardie

K001 Sublime baby cashmere merino silk dk in shade 122 honey bunny	2	3	3	4	50g balls

in garter stitch should measure 10cm, (4in) using 3¾mm needles square when slightly stretched. If your square isn't the correct width please refer to page 2.

ABBREVIATIONS
cm centimetres, **dk** double knitting, **g** grammes, **in** inch(es), **k** knit, **mm** millimetres, **0** no rows, **psso** pass slipped st over, **s1** slip st knitways, **st(s)** stitch(es), **yfwd** yarn forward.
K2tog insert the right hand needle through the 2nd and 1st stitches on the left hand needle and knit them together to form a single stitch.
K2togtbl insert the right hand needle knitways through back of the 1st and 2nd stitches on the left hand needle from left to right and knit them together to form a single stitch.

Circle the size you wish to make

LITTLE PETAL CARDIE
BODY
(Knitted in one piece to armholes)
Using your larger needles cast on

121 [133:143:155] sts.
1st Row. (this will be the right side of the work - **rs**) S1, knit to end.
This row forms garter stitch.
Continue in garter stitch for the remainder of the work as follows:-
Work 6 rows straight.
8th Row. S1, k3, leave these 4 sts on a stitch holder, cast off 113 [125:135:147] sts, k3.
Working on these 4 sts work 18 rows. **Do not break off yarn.**
With wrong side of work facing, rejoin yarn to 4 sts left on a stitch holder and work 18 rows. Break off yarn. Leave these 4 sts on a stitch holder.
Beginning with 4 sts left on needle work as follows:-
Next Row. S1, k3, cast on 105 [117:127:139] sts, knit across 4 sts left on a stitch holder. You will now have 113 [125:135:147] sts on the needle.
Next Row. S1, knit to end.

For 1st size only
1st Row. S1, k29, s1, k2tog, psso, k47, s1,

k2tog, psso, k30. You will now have 109 sts on the needle.
Work 1 row straight.
3rd Row. S1, k28, s1, k2tog, psso, k45, s1, k2tog, psso, k29. You will now have 105 sts on the needle.
Work 1 row straight.
5th Row. S1, k27, s1, k2tog, psso, k43, s1, k2tog, psso, k28. You will now have 101 sts on the needle.
Work 3 rows straight.
9th Row. S1, k27, k2tog, k41, k2tog, k28. You will now have 99 sts on the needle.
Work 5 rows straight.

For 2nd, 3rd and 4th sizes only
1st Row. S1, k[33:35:38], k2tog, k[53:59:65], k2tog, k[34:36:39].
You will now have [123:133:145] sts on the needle.
Work [1:5:7] rows straight.
Next Row. S1, k[32:34:37], k2tog, k[53:59:65], k2tog, k[33:35:38]. You will now have [121:131:143] sts on the needle.
Work [1:5:7] rows straight.
Next Row. S1, k[31:33:36], k2tog, k[53:59:65], k2tog, k[32:34:37]. You will now have [119:129:141] sts on the needle.
Work [3:5:7] rows straight.
Next Row. S1, k[30:32:35], k2tog, k[53:59:65], k2tog, k[31:33:36]. You will now have [117:127:139] sts on the needle.
Work [3:5:7] rows straight.
Next Row. S1, k[29:31:34], k2tog, k[53:59:65], k2tog, k[30:32:35]. You will now have [115:125:137] sts on the needle.
Work [3:5:9] rows straight.
Next Row. S1, k[28:30:33], k2tog, k[53:59:65], k2tog, k[29:31:34]. You will now have [113:123:135] sts on the needle.
Work [3:7:9] rows straight.

For 2nd and 4th sizes only
Next Row. S1, k[27:32], k2tog, k[53:65], k2tog, k[28:33]. You will now have [111:133] sts on the needle.

Work [5:9] rows straight.

For all 4 sizes
Divide for Back and Fronts
Beginning with the right side of the work facing you divide for Back and Fronts as follows:-
Next Row. S1, k22 [25:28:30], k2tog, leave these 24 [27:30:32] sts on a stitch holder. You will come back to these 24 [27:30:32] sts later to work the right front, k2tog, k45 [51:57:63], k2tog, leave these 47 [53:59:65] sts on a stitch holder. You will come back to these 47 [53:59:65] sts later to work the back, k2tog, k23 [26:29:31].
You will now have 24 [27:30:32] sts on the needle.

LEFT FRONT
Working on these 24 [27:30:32] sts proceed as follows:-
1st Row. S1, knit to last 2 sts, k2tog, (armhole edge). You will now have 23 [26:29:31] sts on the needle.
2nd Row. K2tog, knit to end. You will now have 22 [25:28:30] sts on the needle.
Work 3 [5:7:8] rows decreasing 1 st at armhole edge as before in every row. You will now have 19 [20:21:22] sts on the needle.
Continue without shaping until armhole measures 4 [5:6:6]cm, (1½ [2:2½:2½]in), finishing after a right side row.

Neck Shaping
Next Row. Cast off 4 [5:5:5] sts (neck edge), knit to end. You will now have 15 [15:16:17] sts on the needle.
Next Row. S1, knit to last 5 sts, k2tog, k3. You will now have 14 [14:15:16] sts on the needle.
Next Row. S1, k2, k2tog, knit to end. You will now have 13 [13:14:15] sts on the needle.
Work 3 [3:5:3] rows decreasing 1 st at neck edge as before in 1st and every following alternate row.
You will now have 11 [11:11:13] sts on the

needle.
Work 4 [4:8:4] rows decreasing 1 st at neck edge as before in 4th and following 0 [0:4th:0] row.
You will now have 10 [10:9:12] sts on the needle.

For 1st, 2nd and 4th sizes only
Work 6 rows decreasing 1 st at neck edge as before in 6th row. You will now have 9 [9:11] sts on the needle.

For all 4 sizes
Work on these 9 [9:9:11] sts until the armhole measures 10 [11:12:13]cm, (4 [4¼:4¾:5¼]in), straight down from the top of the needle to the beginning of the armhole shaping (don't measure round the curve), finishing after a wrong side row.

Shape Shoulder
Cast off remaining 9 [9:9:11] sts.

BACK
With wrong side facing, rejoin yarn to 47 [53:59:65] sts left on a stitch holder for back and proceed as follows:-
Next Row. K2tog, knit to last 2 sts, k2tog. You will now have 45 [51:57:63] sts on the needle.
Work 4 [6:8:9] rows decreasing 1 st at each end as before in every row. You will now have 37 [39:41:45] sts on the needle.
Work without shaping until back armholes measure same as Left Front armhole to shoulder shaping, finishing after a wrong side row.

Shape Shoulder
Cast off remaining 37 [39:41:45] sts placing a marker to indicate back of neck at each side of centre 19 [21:23:23] sts.

RIGHT FRONT
With wrong side facing, rejoin yarn to 24 [27:30:32] sts left on a stitch holder for right front

and proceed as follows:-
1st Row. K2tog (armhole edge), knit to end. You will now have 23 [26:29:31] sts on the needle.
2nd Row. S1, knit to last 2 sts, k2tog. You will now have 22 [25:28:30] sts on the needle.
Work 3 [5:7:8] rows decreasing 1 st at armhole edge as before in every row. You will now have 19 [20:21:22] sts on the needle.
Work without shaping until front edge is 4 rows less than Left Front to neck, finishing after a wrong side row.
Next Row. (buttonhole row) S1, k2, k2tog, yfwd, knit to end.
Work 3 rows straight.

Neck Shaping
Next Row. Cast off 4 [5:5:5] sts, (neck edge) knit to end. You will now have 15 [15:16:17] sts on the needle.
Next Row. S1, knit to end.
Next Row. S1, k2, k2togtbl, knit to end. You will now have 14 [14:15:16] sts on the needle.
Next Row. S1, knit to last 5 sts, k2togtbl, k3. You will now have 13 [13:14:15] sts on the needle.
Work 3 [3:5:3] rows decreasing 1 st at neck edge as before in 1st and every following alternate row.
You will now have 11 [11:11:13] sts on the needle.
Work 4 [4:8:4] rows decreasing 1 st at neck edge as before in 4th and following 0 [0:4th:0] row.
You will now have 10 [10:9:12] sts on the needle.

For 1st, 2nd and 4th sizes only
Work 6 rows decreasing 1 st at neck edge as before in 6th row. You will now have 9 [9:11] sts on the needle.

For all 4 sizes
Work straight until right front armhole measures same as back armhole to shoulder shaping, finishing after a right side row.

Shape Shoulder
Cast off remaining 9 [9:9:11] sts.

SLEEVES (Both alike)
Using your larger needles cast on 36 [36: 38:40] sts.
1st Row. (this will be the right side of the work - **rs**) S1, knit to end.
Work in garter stitch for the remainder of the sleeve as follows:-
Work 52 [58:52:52] rows increasing 1 st at each end of 4th and every following 48th [18th:16th:16th] row (there will be 47 [17: 15:15] rows straight between each increase row).
You will now have 40 [44:46:48] sts on the needle.

For 3rd and 4th sizes only
Work [18:36] rows increasing 1 st at each end of 18th and following [0:18th] row (there will be 17 rows straight between each increase row). You will now have [48:52] sts on the needle.

For all 4 sizes
Work without further shaping until the sleeve is 15 [17:20:24]cm, (6 [6½:8:9½]in), finishing after a wrong side row.

Shape Sleeve Top
Work 6 [8:10:11] rows decreasing 1 st at each end of every row. You will now have 28 [28: 28:30] sts on the needle. Place marker threads at each end of last row. These 6 [8:10:11] rows will match to the 6 [8:10:11] decrease rows on body when sewing the sleeves into armhole.
Work 0 [0:0:1] rows straight.
Cast off 1 [2:1:2] sts at the beginning of each of the next 4 [10:4:8] rows.
You will now have 24 [8:24:14] sts on the needle.

For 1st, 3rd and 4th sizes only
Cast off 2 [2:3] sts at the beginning of each of the next 8 [8:2] rows.
You will now have 8 [8:8] sts on the needle.

For all 4 sizes
Cast off remaining 8 sts.

FLOWERS
Using your smaller needles cast on 66 sts.
1st Row. (K1, cast off 9 sts) 6 times. You will now have 12 sts on the needle.
Draw yarn through remaining 12 sts.
Fasten off.
Make 12 [14:15:16] flowers.

TO MAKE UP
Join side and sleeve seams. Sew sleeve tops into armholes matching the 6 [8:10:11] decrease rows on the body to the 6 [8:10:11] decrease rows marked at the beginning of the sleeve top. Attach flowers to cast off and cast on edges in body opening, joining flowers to each other where petals meet. Sew on button. Pin out garment to the measurement given. Cover with damp cloths and leave until dry (refer to page 2). See ball band for washing and further care instructions.

PEACH PETAL CARDIE
BODY
Work the body as given for Body of Little Petal Cardie.

SLEEVES (Both alike)
Using your larger needles cast on 36 [40: 44:48] sts.
1st Row. (this will be the right side of the work - **rs**) S1, knit to end.
Work in garter stitch for the remainder of the sleeve as follows:-
Work 3 rows straight.

Shape Sleeve Top
Work 6 [8:10:11] rows decreasing 1 st at each end of every row. You will now have 24 [24:

24:26] sts on the needle. Place marker threads at each end of last row. These 6 [8:10:11] rows will match to the 6 [8:10:11] decrease rows on body when sewing the sleeves into armhole.

Work 0 [0:0:1] rows straight.

Cast off 1 st at the beginning of each of the next 16 [12:16:10] rows.

You will now have 8 [12:8:16] sts on the

needle.

For 2nd and 4th sizes only

Cast off 2 sts at the beginning of each of the next [2:4] rows. You will now have [8:8] sts on the needle.

For all 4 sizes

Cast off remaining 8 sts.

FLOWERS

Work the flowers as given for Flowers of Little Petal Cardie.

TO MAKE UP

Work to make up as given for To Make Up of Little Petal Cardie.

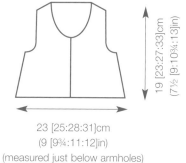

23 [25:28:31]cm
(9 [9¾:11:12]in)
(measured just below armholes)

19 [23:27:33]cm
(7½ [9:10¾:13]in)

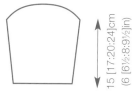

15 [17:20:24]cm
(6 [6½:8:9½]in)

1cm
(½in)

Sublime™

Candy Stripe and Little Candy

worked in Sublime baby
cashmere merino silk dk

You will also need
1 pair of 4mm (UK8 – USA6) Knitting
Needles (or the size required to give the
correct tension).
1 pair of 3¼mm (UK10 – USA3) Knitting
Needles for the edgings (or a needle 2 sizes
smaller than you use for the main knitting).
Stitch holders.

TENSION
Please take a little time now to knit a stocking
stitch tension square. **Using 4mm needles
cast on 22 stitches and work 28 rows in
stocking stitch (1 row knit, 1 row purl). This
should now measure 10cm, (4in) square.** If
your square isn't the correct width please refer
to page 2.

SIZES

Age	0-6 months	6-12 months	1-2 years	2-3 years	
To Fit Chest	41	46	51	56	cm
	16	18	20	22	in
Actual Size	41	46	52	55	cm
	16	18	20½	21¾	in
Full Length)	16	17	21	25	cm
(approximately	6¼	6½	8¼	9¾	in
Sleeve Length					
(adjustable) Little Candy	15	17	20	24	cm
	6	6½	8	9½	in
Candy Stripe	0.5	0.5	0.5	0.5	cm
	¼	¼	¼	¼	in

MATERIALS
Candy Stripe
K001 Sublime baby cashmere merino silk dk

shade 126 rosy for main	1	1	1	2	50g balls
shade 121 mousse for contrast	1	1	1	2	50g balls

Little Candy
K001 Sublime baby cashmere merino silk dk

shade 126 rosy	2	2	3	3	50g balls

ABBREVIATIONS
cm centimetres, **dk** double knitting,
g grammes, **in** inch(es), **k** knit, **mm** millimetres,
0 no stitches, times or rows, **p** purl,
st(s) stitch(es), **tog** together.
K2tog insert the right hand needle through the
2nd and 1st stitches on the left hand needle
and knit them together to form a single stitch.
P2tog insert the right hand needle purlways
through the 1st and 2nd stitches on the left
hand needle and purl them together to form a
single stitch.
Psso pass slipped stitch over – pass the
slipped stitch from right hand needle over the
stitch or stitches you have just worked.
S1 slip 1 stitch knitways - insert the right hand
needle into the next stitch as if to knit but just
slip it off the left hand needle onto the right
needle without working.

Circle the size you wish to make

CANDY STRIPE
Stripe Sequence
1st and 2nd Rows. Using main, work 2 rows.
3rd and 4th Rows. Using contrast, work 2
rows.

BACK
Using your main needles and main, cast on
39 [45:51:55] sts.
1st Row (this will be the right side of
work – **rs**). Knit.
This row forms garter stitch.
Work 1 row more in garter stitch.
Beginning with a knit row and using contrast,
work 2 rows in stocking stitch.
Work in stocking stitch and stripe sequence
for the remainder of the back as follows:-

Work 9 [9:15:15] rows increasing 1 st at each end of 1st [1st:3rd:3rd] and every following 4th [4th:6th:6th] row. You will now have 45 [51:57:61] sts on the needle.
Work 5 [5:7:15] rows straight.
The back should measure approximately 20 [23:26:28]cm, (8 [9:10¼:11]in) across at this point.

Shape Armholes
Work 4 [6:7:7] rows decreasing 1 st at each end of every row. You will now have 37 [39:43:47] sts on the needle.
Work on these 37 [39:43:47] sts until the armholes measure 10 [11:12:13]cm, (4 [4¼:4¾:5¼]in), straight down from top of the needle to the beginning of the armhole shaping (don't measure around the curve), finishing after a purl row.

Shape Shoulders
Cast off 6 [6:7:8] sts at beginning of next 2 rows. You will now have 25 [27:29:31] sts on the needle.
Cast off 6 [7:7:8] sts at beginning of next 2 rows. You will now have 13 [13:15:15] sts on the needle.
Cast off remaining 13 [13:15:15] sts.

TIES (Both alike)
Using your smaller needles and main, cast on 21 sts.
Work 2 rows in garter stitch.
Change to your main needles. Beginning with a knit row and using contrast, work 2 rows in stocking stitch.
Work in stocking stitch and stripe sequence as follows:-
Work 12 [12:4:4] rows decreasing 1 st at each end of 1st and every following 4th [4th:0:0] row. You will now have 15 [15:19:19] sts on the needle.
Work 16 [16:28:28] rows decreasing 1 st at each end of 1st and every following 6th row. You will now have 9 sts on the needle. **
Leave these 9 sts on a stitch holder.

LEFT FRONT
Using your main needles and main, cast on 11 [14:17:19] sts.
1st Row. Knit to end, knit across 9 sts left on a stitch holder for left tie. You will now have 20 [23:26:28] sts on the needle.
2nd Row. P9, k11 [14:17:19].
3rd Row. Using contrast, knit to last 5 sts, k2tog, k3 (front edge). You will now have 19 [22:25:27] sts on the needle.
This row sets front edge decreases.
4th Row. Purl.
Working in stocking stitch and stripe sequence for the remainder of the left front, work 0 [0:2:2] rows more.
Next Row. Increase in 1st st (side edge), knit to end. You will now have 20 [23:26:28] sts on the needle.
This row sets side edge increases.
Next Row. Purl.
Work 10 [10:16:16] rows increasing 1 st at side edge in 3rd [3rd:5th:5th] and following 4th [4th:6th:6th] row AT SAME TIME decreasing 1 st at front edge as before in 9th [9th:7th:9th] row. You will now have 21 [24:27:29] sts on the needle.
Work 2 [2:2:10] rows decreasing 1 st at front edge only in 0 [0:0:7th] row. You will now have 21 [24:27:28] sts on the needle.

Shape Armhole
1st Row. K2tog (armhole edge), knit to last 0 [0:5:0] sts, (k2tog, k3) 0 [0:1:0] times. You will now have 20 [23:25:27] sts on the needle.
2nd Row. Purl to last 2 sts, p2tog. You will now have 19 [22:24:26] sts on the needle.
These 2 rows set armhole shaping.
Work 2 [4:5:5] rows more decreasing 1 st at armhole edge in every row. You will now have 17 [18:19:21] sts on the needle.
Work 17 [17:18:18] rows decreasing 1 st at neck edge only as before in 5th [3rd:6th:4th] and following 12th [14th:12th:14th] row. You will now have 15 [16:17:19] sts on the needle.

For all 4 sizes
Work straight until left front armhole measures same as Back armhole to shoulder shaping, finishing after a purl row.

Shape Shoulder
Next Row. Cast off 6 [6:7:8] sts, knit to end. You will now have 9 [10:10:11] sts on the needle.
Next Row. Purl.
Next Row. Cast off 6 [7:7:8] sts, knit to end. You will now have 3 sts on the needle.
Next Row. Purl to end, cast on 1 st (this st will be used to sew back neck border to the back neck). You will now have 4 sts on the needle.

Back Neck Border
Continue on these 4 sts until back neck border is of sufficient length to go to centre back of neck, finishing after a purl row.
Cast off.

RIGHT FRONT
Using your main needles and main, cast on 11 [14:17:19] sts. Break off yarn.
1st Row. With rs facing and using main knit across 9 sts left on stitch holder for right tie then across 11 [14:17:19] cast on sts. You will now have 20 [23:26:28] sts on the needle.
2nd Row. K11 [14:17:19], p9.
3rd Row. Using contrast, k3, s1, k1, psso (front edge), knit to end. You will now have 19 [22:25:27] sts on the needle.
This row sets front edge decreases.
4th Row. Purl.
Working in stocking stitch and stripe sequence for the remainder of the right front, work 0 [0:2:2] rows more.
Next Row. Knit to last 2 sts, increase in next st, k1 (side edge). You will now have 20 [23:26:28] sts on the needle.
This row sets side edge increases.
Next Row. Purl.
Work 10 [10:16:16] rows decreasing 1 st at front edge as before in 9th [9th:7th:9th] row AT SAME TIME increasing 1 st at side edge in

3rd [3rd:5th:5th] and following 4th [4th:6th:6th] row. You will now have 21 [24:27:29] sts on the needle.
Work 2 [2:2:10] rows decreasing 1 st at front edge only in 0 [0:0:7th] row. You will now have 21 [24:27:28] sts on the needle.

Shape Armhole

1st Row. (K3, s1, k1, psso) 0 [0:1:0] times, knit to last 2 sts, k2tog (armhole edge). You will now have 20 [23:25:27] sts on the needle.
2nd Row. P2tog, purl to end. You will now have 19 [22:24:26] sts on the needle.
These 2 rows set armhole shaping.
Work 2 [4:5:5] rows more decreasing 1 st at armhole edge in every row. You will now have 17 [18:19:21] sts on the needle.
Work 17 [17:18:18] rows decreasing 1 st at neck edge only as before in 5th [3rd:6th:4th] and following 12th [14th:12th:14th] row. You will now have 15 [16:17:19] sts on the needle.

For all 4 sizes

Work straight until right front armhole measures same as Back armhole to shoulder shaping, finishing after a knit row.

Shape Shoulder

Next Row. Cast off 6 [6:7:8] sts, purl to end. You will now have 9 [10:10:11] sts on the needle.
Next Row. Knit.
Next Row. Cast off 6 [7:7:8] sts, purl to end. You will now have 3 sts on the needle.
Next Row. Knit to end, cast on 1 st (this st will be used to sew back neck border to the back neck). You will now have 4 sts on the needle. Continue on these 4 sts until back neck border is of sufficient length to go to centre back of neck finishing after a purl row.
Cast off.

SLEEVES (Both alike)

Using your smaller needles and main, cast on 31 [36:40:44] sts.

Work 2 rows in garter stitch.
Change to your main needles. Starting with a knit row and using contrast, continue in stocking stitch and stripe sequence for the remainder of the sleeve as follows:-

Shape Sleeve Top

Work 4 [6:7:7] rows decreasing 1 st at each end of every row. You will now have 23 [24: 26:30] sts on the needle. These 4 [6:7:7] rows will match to 4 [6:7:7] decrease rows on body when sewing the sleeves into armholes.
Work 2 [2:3:3] rows straight.
Work 4 rows decreasing 1 st at each end of 1st and 3rd row. You will now have 19 [20: 22:26] sts on the needle.
Work 2 [2:2:4] rows decreasing 1 st at each end of every row. You will now have 15 [16: 18:18] sts on the needle.
Cast off 3 [3:4:4] sts at beginning of next 2 rows. You will now have 9 [10:10:10] sts on the needle.
Cast off remaining 9 [10:10:10] sts.

TO MAKE UP

Join both shoulder, side and sleeve seams. Sew sleeve tops into armholes matching the 4 [6:7:7] decrease rows on the body to the 4 [6:7:7] decrease rows at the beginning of the sleeve top. Join cast off edges of back neck border together then sew back neck border to back of neck. Pin out garment to the measurement given and cover with damp cloths until dry (refer to page 2). See ball band for washing and further care instructions.

LITTLE CANDY
BACK

Work the back as given for Back of Candy Stripe, using 1 colour only.

LEFT FRONT

Work the left front as given for Left Front of Candy Stripe, using 1 colour only.

RIGHT FRONT

Work the right front as given for Right Front of Candy Stripe, using 1 colour only.

SLEEVES (Both alike)

Using your smaller needles cast on 32 [32: 34:34] sts.
Work 2 rows in garter stitch.
Change to your main needles and starting with a knit row work in stocking stitch for the remainder of the sleeve as follows:-
Work 13 [29:35:47] rows increasing 1 st at each end of 5th and every following 8th [6th: 6th:6th] row (there will be 7 [5:5:5] rows straight between each increase row). You will now have 36 [42:46:50] sts on the needle.
Work 20 [8:8:8] rows increasing 1 st at each end of every following 10th [8th:8th:8th] row (there will 9 [7:7:7] rows straight between each increase row). You will now have 40 [44:48:52] sts on the needle.
Work without further shaping until the sleeve is 15 [17:20:24]cm, (6 [6½:8:9½]in), or length required, finishing after a purl row.

Shape Sleeve Top

Work 4 [6:7:7] rows decreasing 1 st at each end of every row. You will now have 32 [32: 34:38] sts on the needle.
These 4 [6:7:7] rows will match to 4 [6:7:7] decrease rows on body when sewing the sleeves into armholes.
Work 0 [0:1:1] rows without shaping.
Cast off 2 [3:3:3] sts at beginning of each of the next 2 [2:2:6] rows. You will now have 28 [26:28:20] sts on the needle.
Cast off 3 [4:4:4] sts at beginning of each of the next 6 [4:4:2] rows. You will now have 10 [10:12:12] sts on the needle.
Cast off remaining 10 [10:12:12] sts.

TO MAKE UP

Work to make up as given for To Make Up of Candy Stripe.

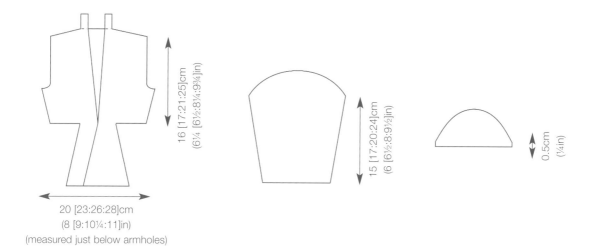

16 [17:21:25]cm
(6¼ [6½:8¼:9¾]in)

20 [23:26:28]cm
(8 [9:10¼:11]in)
(measured just below armholes)

15 [17:20:24]cm
(6 [6½:8:9½]in)

0.5cm
(¼in)

NOTES

Pretty as a peach in this cute little cover up –
it looks gorgeous with pretty summer dresses
or pantaloons.
Peach Sorbet Cardie

Just to show you this easy flower pattern goes
all the way around the cardie.
Peach Petal Cardie
Little Petal Alice Band

This little tie front cardie striped in two of our prettiest pinks is a quick weekend knit.
Candy Stripe

You will love knitting this quick and easy cardie – choose your colours and knit one to go with each of their favourite frocks.
Little Candy

Knit a simple Alice Band to
go with your cardie for the
glamorous girlie effect.
Little Sorbet Cardie
Alice Band

Sublime™

For that sporty nautical look, team
this little knit with white linen shorts.
Big Anchor Man
Little Anchor Beanie

Perfect for wearing with t-shirts and shorts
for those holidays by the sea.
Blue Anchor Man

A great hat for blustery boat rides. He could
sail around the world in this one – or maybe
just around the park.
Little Anchor Beanie

This pretty little cardie with its Sublime flower details looks more complicated than it is – these are just the easiest flowers to knit (we give you great instructions!) Try it this weekend.
Little Petal Cardie

This sunny little cardie will pretty up the
most simple summer frocks. Add the
Alice band for the full flower fairy effect.
Sunflower Cardie
Sunflower Alice Band

Long or short sleeved, this gorgeously versatile little cardie is a must have for every baby girl's wardrobe.
Peach Petal Cardie
Little Petal Alice Band

Other Sublime books

600 - The little Sublime
hand knit book

601 - The very gorgeous
Sublime kid mohair book

602 - The Sublime merino
hand knit book

603 - The most luxurious
Sublime hand knit book

604 - The Sublime aran
hand knit book

605 - The very stylish
Sublime angora merino book

606 - The second little
Sublime hand knit book

607 - The Sublime double
knitting book

608 - The second Sublime
aran hand knit book

609 - The even more gorgeous
Sublime kid mohair book

610 - The luxuriously exotic
soya cotton hand knit book

611 - The simply Sublime
organic cotton dk book

612 - The third little Sublime
hand knit book

613 - The Sublime children's
double knitting book

614 - The exquisitely soft Sublime
organic merino wool book

615 - The third Sublime
Aran hand knit book

616 - The irresistibly Sublime
Baby 4 Ply Book

617 - The fourth little
Sublime hand knit book

Sublime™

Sublime
a greatness with which nothing else can be compared and is beyond all possibility of calculation, measurement and imitation.

617

Mixed Sources
Product group from well-managed forests, and other controlled sources
www.fsc.org Cert no. CU-COC-809387
© 1996 Forest Stewardship Council
FSC

Sublime™ Flanshaw Lane Wakefield West Yorkshire WF2 9ND United Kingdom
t +44 [0]1924 369666 **f** +44 [0]1924 290506 **e** contactus@sublimeyarns.com
The Sublime knitting helpline: +44 [0]1924 231686

Sublime is a Trade Mark of Sirdar Spinning Limited

Ref: WP61